The Personal Statement Method

THE PERSONAL STATEMENT METHOD

THE FUSS-FREE GUIDE TO WRITING A SUCCESSFUL

UCAS PERSONAL STATEMENT

ALEX J BENT

Faulkner
Colvin
Education

Published by
Faulkner Colvin Education Ltd.
Kemp House,
160 City Road,
London,
EC1V 2NX
UK
Tel: (+44) 020 8638 5504
contact@faulknercolvineducation.co.uk

First published: 2019

Print Edition   ISBN 978 1 9160798 0 9
eBook Edition   ISBN 978 1 9160798 1 6

CONTENTS

INTRODUCTION

What is this book?

This book is your guide to writing a better UCAS Personal Statement. It is your guide to crafting a successful application to the UK's most competitive university courses. Like most Personal Statement books, it's designed to help you with the planning, preparation, writing, checking and editing of your Personal Statement. But it's also different to most Personal Statement books. Most will tell you how to focus on you and bring out the best parts of yourself; this one goes further than that. This book is different because it encourages you to think about not just what you can show, but to think about and understand exactly what universities are looking for. Through studying and understanding the courses at the universities you're applying to, this book helps you to raise the level of your Personal Statement by helping you write not just about yourself, but to write about why you are the best person for the university and course that you're applying for. Why should they choose you above all others?

It also guides you in turning each of the activities you plan to write about into valuable learning points that demonstrate your abilities to engage with your subjects, reflect on your activities, and reinforce the links between yourself and your future. That's what makes it different. That's what makes your Personal Statement better. That's what gets you offers from the most competitive courses.

Who is this book for?

If you're sitting down to write your Personal Statement and you've no idea what to write - this book is for you. It will give you a method to think about the kind of things you need to demonstrate and show you how you can include them in your Personal Statement.

If you've some idea what to write but you want to make your Personal Statement one of the best that the admissions officers will read this year - this book is also for you. It will guide you through structure, examples, reflections, writing, and editing. It will help you to avoid common clichés and faux pas. It will help you to eradicate the slips and annoyances complained about by admissions officers. It will help you to make your Personal Statement better.

If you're a hands-on parent, grandparent or teacher looking to help the students in your life - this book is not for you, but you still might find some useful guidance and insights that will help you to ensure a bright future for your young charges.

What are we going to talk about?

The main part of this book is divided into the five major stages of preparing and writing your Personal Statement: Understanding Your Course, Organising Your Experiences, Reflections, Writing the Statement, and Editing.

Step 1: Understanding Your Course

In this chapter you'll investigate exactly what each university is hoping to see in its applicants. We'll discuss the key criteria cited by admissions officers, and what that means for you. As we work through each of the possible areas and skills that are required by institutes of higher learning, you'll get a better understanding of why these are important and which courses require what skills. Whilst we'll discuss some of the main skills for some of the main courses, you'll also discover how you can find out what you specifically need for your course at your university. There'll be no need for guess work - universities make this information available if you know where to look and know how to read it.

Step 2: Organising Your Experiences - The Importance of Examples

This is where we start to think more about you and the things that you've done over the past few years. We'll talk about structure and what we mean by "Academic", "Super-Curricular" and "Extra-Curricular" examples as well as the areas you should focus on most when writing your Personal Statement. This section is also laden with "examples of examples" from previously successful Personal Statements to give you some ideas about the types of things that other students have done and how they have written about them.

Step 3: Reflections

This is where we take your Personal Statement to the next level. The Reflections chapter shows you the importance of being able to reflect on what you've done and what you've achieved, as well as giving you some simple tricks to make a difficult process easy. Using the Authenticity Questions from this chapter, you'll be able to move your Personal Statement from one that's bland, generic, and uninspired, to one that gets admissions officers to sit up and take notice of you.

Step 4: Writing the Statement

After the previous three chapters, what previously seemed like the hardest thing in the world (writing your Personal Statement) will now seem like a breeze, and you'll be eager to get on with it. It's certainly worth pausing to read this chapter first though, as it will go through some great ways to begin and end your statement, help you in structuring your individual paragraphs and show you some common errors that you need to avoid, as well as how to make your Personal Statement more engaging through the use of active language.

Step 5: Editing

We're heading towards the end game now, by the time you reach this chapter you'll have the first draft of your Personal Statement in place and will be ready to polish it to a shine. Focusing in on the technicalities of spelling, grammar and style, as well as getting your word count under control and giving you some suggestions on the best ways to get your Personal Statement checked, the fifth and final chapter is the one that makes your Personal Statement application ready. After this, you'll be ready to send it.

Appendix 1: Complete Personal Statement Examples

Still not had enough and want to see some examples? Appendix 1 has 11 real examples of Personal Statements that had great success for their writers. In the appendix, you'll find complete and authentic Personal Statement examples for Engineering, Mathematics and Statistics, Business, Marketing, English and Creative Writing, Liberal Arts, Psychology, International Relations, Computer Science, Economics, and Medicine.

Appendix 2: Planning and Writing Worksheets

At the end of each chapter you'll be called upon to complete a specific task or activity that will help you in your planning, preparation or writing. In Appendix 2 you'll find some nifty worksheets to help you with these, as well as a checklist of questions both for yourself and for those who you ask to help you during the editing process.

How should you use this book?

There are two ways to work with this book: the quick way, and the normal way. Whilst you're perfectly free to put the book down and complete the activities when the book tells you to (and indeed it has been designed for this), if you're like most people you'll probably want to read the whole things first to see where you're going, and then come back to reread each chapter and complete the activities. There are two rules you do need to follow however:

1) You do need to do all the activities that the book tells you to do - there's no point buying a book if you don't take action.

2) You need to do them in order - the thought processes and activities are specifically designed to scaffold you through the process of researching, planning, writing and editing your statement. Resist the temptation to bounce around; you're better to follow the path laid out.

Getting on the same page - essential understandings before we begin

Before we get into all that though, we need to make sure that we're all on the same page about what a Personal Statement is, and what it is not.

Your UCAS Personal Statement makes up just one part of your application to all UK universities. Alongside your Personal Statement, you'll also need to send the rest of the application form (personal details and past grades), your Predicted Grades (this is for your school to complete) and your school reference (again, to be done by your school). What this means is that, whilst your Personal Statement is certainly of great importance, it is just one part of the application. A fantastic Personal Statement cannot make up for poor Predicted Grades. If your university is asking for A*AA at A-Level, and your Predicted Grades are BCC, even the best Personal Statement will not be able to bridge that gap. Your Personal Statement will come into play when you're being considered against candidates who have similar grades to you and will be used as the differentiating factor when places are limited.

But what is it? Simply put, it's a 4000-character statement about yourself and your reasons for wanting to study your chosen course. It's about why you are the best candidate for the course. Importantly, the 4000-character limit includes spaces - and there are no exceptions.

Another important thing to note, is that when applying to UK universities, you may only submit one Personal Statement. On UCAS you can choose up to 5 choices of universities and courses, but you'll be sending the same Personal Statement to each of them. This means that you need to be very careful in selecting your courses; realistically you should be applying for the same course at 5 different universities. You can only write one Personal Statement, and it needs to be tailored to the course. If you attempt to apply for 5 different courses, or even just two dissimilar courses, this makes your Personal Statement almost impossible to write and greatly reduces your chances of success.

Your Personal Statement needs to show your passion for your chosen course. It should demonstrate to universities that studying your course is a decision you've thought through and been working towards. Universities do not want half-hearted students who are there simply for the name of the institution or the city, they want students who live and breathe their courses and who will actively seek out opportunities to succeed and excel. This is what your Personal Statement is. This is what your Personal Statement needs to show. It needs to show your passion for something that you're going to spend the next three or four years of your life studying. It also needs to show that you have the skills and abilities to match that passion.

These are the tenets of a great Personal Statement - one that evidences your passion and skills for your future course. The rest of this book will guide you to demonstrating this in the best way possible, but before you can do that, we must start with understanding exactly what each different course will be looking for in its candidates. Bring on Step 1.

STEP 1:

UNDERSTANDING YOUR COURSE

Before you can even think about what's going to make a good personal statement, you need to completely and thoroughly understand the course you are applying for. If you understand your course, you can work out exactly what characteristics the admissions officer wants to see in an ideal student. That way, you know what characteristics you need to show that you possess in your Personal Statement. Once you have these, you can use them as the baseline and the structure for your Personal Statement.

This chapter will help you to understand some of the main characteristics that universities require, before showing you how to go through the process of discovering this information from the course websites and from the module guides. To make life even easier, it summarises some of the most common characteristics needed for the most popular courses, but this list is not exhaustive and it's still a good idea to back this up with your own research.

It may be tempting to skip this chapter and move straight to writing. Don't.

A little preparation work now could save you hours in the long run: understand your course, understand what they want to see, understand how you need to present yourself.

What do universities want to see?

A look at the data:

According to the University Admissions Officers Report 2015, published by ACS International Schools, beyond your academic qualifications and your grades, there are 5 key general areas that admissions officers are looking for in all their candidates:

- 93% said they were looking to see "a passion for the chosen subject"

- 93% said they wanted "good written English"

- 92% needed to be sure "that a candidate could complete their degree"

- 86% wanted evidence of a positive attitude towards study

- 72% wanted to see that a candidate could think and work independently

You might be surprised to know that your skills and experience in organising clubs and societies was taken into account by only 6% of admissions officers. This doesn't mean your time spent on these was wasted, but it does have implications for your Personal Statement. It's not about what you did. It's about what you learnt from this and how you can apply it to success in your chosen course. This fact is so important that it's worth repeating again and again: your statement must be built around your suitability for the course

There are some points you need to mention implicitly, rather than stating them explicitly. For example, as mentioned earlier, your passion for the subject should be flowing throughout your statement. In every point and every paragraph, you'll be demonstrating your passion clearly and proudly. We'll focus on how to do that when we start generating examples in Step 2. Similarly, your written English is on display throughout your statement, so unless you're applying for an English course, you won't need to write a paragraph about it. Again, we'll focus on that during Step 5 when we look at the editing and review process.

That leaves us with three general points to make sure we cover:

- "Positive attitude towards study"
- "Thinking and working independently"
- "Your ability to complete your degree"

So, what do we mean by each of these?

Positive attitude towards study

This links with the idea of passion for your course. You can show it through the areas where you've independently gone "beyond" your course. If you're reading widely, or attending events, lectures, and competitions relevant to your subject, this shows your positive attitude. You may not need to devote a specific paragraph to this, but ensure it is highlighted at relevant opportunities. If you're only completing the work that you've been set by your teacher, this doesn't necessarily show a positive attitude – it might just show a fear of your teacher!

Thinking and working independently

At university, this is something that you're expected to do. No one is going to chase you for essays or to do your reading before your seminars. If you don't do it, you don't do it. But if you don't do it, you perform poorly and put yourself at risk of failure. No university wants to take a student only to have them fail. Thinking and working independently is crucial and could be worth a paragraph in its own right. You can show it through your projects and assignments, any research you've done, anywhere that you've taken initiative and seen something through. Even if you were working as a group, you didn't do everything together. What was your role in the group? What unique piece of the puzzle did you bring to the table and contribute?

Your ability to complete your degree

No university wants to see you fail. That's bad for their reputation, their statistics, and their bank accounts. A key indicator that you'll be able to complete your degree is your grades. This could be your Predicted Grades or past exam grades, which is one reason that it's important that these are strong. Grades show the academic calibre of the student, and good grades now are a good predictor of good grades in the future. Unless there is a very real and legitimate reason why your past grades were low, a university has no reason to believe your promises that "I'll study harder! I'll do better!", they'll just move on to a candidate who has already proven that they can. Even if you have the grades, this doesn't guarantee success in the course. Each course has different needs of its students and their skillsets and an ability to show these in your Personal Statement will go a long way towards convincing the admissions officer that you can complete the course.

What do we mean by different skillsets?

An Art Student or a Product Designer needs to show creativity; this seems a pretty reasonable expectation. Creativity in a History Student however would at best be less important, and at worst could lead to a "creative interpretation" of historical facts – known otherwise as "just making it up". It's not that History Students must not be creative, but it would be a mistake for this to be your main point of emphasis in your Personal Statement. History Students need to be able to prove that they can understand and respond to complex written and verbal arguments. Engineers need to show their comfort with processes and logical thinking. Chemistry Students would benefit from highlighting their research and experimentation skills. Each course is different, each has different needs; you need to show how you meet these needs.

Some of the common skills required

Critical Thinking

This is your ability to apply reasoning and logic to unfamiliar ideas and situations. Thinking critically requires you to come at a problem from a number of different ways in order to better understand and then make progress with an idea or concept. It's relevant to almost all degree courses, though perhaps in different ways. Both Humanities and Science courses for example will need students to be able to take a problem and then think critically about it to come first to a better understanding, and then to a conclusion.

Problem Solving

As expected, this is your ability to solve problems. Strong problem solving requires an ability to understand the goal of the problem and then to work through a series of steps in order to achieve this goal. Being able to describe to an admissions officer of a problem that you had, and the steps and thought processes undertaken to solve it would be a valuable addition to Personal Statements that require this.

Intellectual Curiosity

Are you genuinely interested in taking your understanding further? Someone who is intellectually curious will be going beyond their normal studies and constantly trying to find out more. This could be through asking questions, doing extra reading, attending lectures and seminars, or even conducting projects and experiments in an area that has caught your attention. There are many ways to show your curiosity, but generally, they involve showing where you've pushed something further than the bare minimum you were required to by your current studies.

Creativity

This is not just the ability to dream up new ideas, but also the ability to discover new ways to approach existing things. Creativity can be shown through the creation of physical products such as inventions, works of literature or paintings, but also through concepts, ideas or theories. Creative people are often seen as assets and help to generate new ideas to take discussions in new directions.

Logical thinking

This is about your ability to work with facts and processes, rather than emotions and perspectives, in order to solve problems. A logical thinker will be able to follow the chain of facts clearly to come up with well supported conclusions, theories and ideas.

Ability to see multiple perspectives

Does the idea that two opposing arguments can both be right at the same time frighten you or excite you? Being able to understand two different opposing viewpoints, where they come from and how they are supported is an important skill in a world where there is often no one right answer. This is of particular relevance to Humanities students who will often need to understand ideas and opinions that differ from their own.

Research

The further you go through the levels of a university, the more about research it becomes. Even at an undergraduate level you will be expected to complete a research dissertation, and an understanding of the processes of research will help convince admissions officers that you are suited to university study. Research is a systematic inquiry that can be used to describe, explain, control and predict a phenomenon. It is relevant to all academic subjects and being able to show your experience and understanding of research will benefit all Personal Statements.

Self-Reflectiveness

No one is good at everything. No one is bad at everything. Sometimes things go well. Sometimes things go badly. Being able to reflect upon what went right and wrong, and what your strengths and weaknesses are is a useful skill for students to have. If you're able to reflect upon your weaknesses and then take steps to improve them, this will show a university a potential student who is seeking to better themselves and so has potential for greatness. When you're writing your Personal Statement, it seems obvious to write about things that have gone well and things that you're good at. Sometimes however, it can be even more powerful to identify where something has gone wrong, what it taught you, and the steps you took next.

Participation and engagement

Universities like students who are seeking to be involved and push themselves. Universities do not like students who sit there quietly waiting to be spoon-fed knowledge. They want you to participate and engage both within your course and outside in university life. A good Personal Statement will show how you have actively participated in your education so far and how you contribute to a lively and engaging academic environment.

Communication and relationships

You're going to need to work in groups and small teams when you're at university; your tutors need to know that you're capable of working with others to produce positive results and that when you work with others, the product is greater than the sum of its parts. Being able to show when you've worked in and led small teams through projects at school will help to reassure universities that you're a socially competent individual. More than this, some courses may require more specific communication skills – some require at least basic ability with giving presentations, others rely on your ability to develop and convey clear and structured arguments, both verbally and in writing.

Time management and organisation

If you miss your deadlines, you're going to fail. No one chases you, no one reminds you, no one gives you second/third/fourth/fifth chances to submit your work or study for that exam. It's your responsibility to balance multiple demands. You'll have many different modules and assignments, and many different things to do outside of class. It's a minimum expectation that you can handle this, so it's helpful to prove that you can.

Affinity with numbers

For some courses, you're going to need mathematical skills and an ability to work with numbers. You may need to work with formulae, numerical data sets or other maths-based skills. If maths terrifies you but it's an essential skill, you may need to think about another course.

Empathy

This is the ability to put yourself into someone else's shoes; the ability to understand someone from their own frame of reference. In many ways this is similar to being able to understand multiple perspectives, but on a more personal level. If you're selecting a subject or future career where you're likely to work closely with people and individuals, being able to empathise with others is essential.

Which of these skills are essential to me?

These skills are all clearly very general, could be applied to any Personal Statement and indeed an ideal student will possess all of them. Some are more important to particular courses than others however, and the next few pages are dedicated to highlighting the most important skills for some of the most commonly applied to subjects. To be clear, just because the skill isn't listed below doesn't mean it's not useful and shouldn't be written about. The lists below only highlight the absolute essentials. Once you've identified the essentials for you, you can then start to introduce the others as necessary.

What to do if your course isn't listed? Don't worry. The rest of this chapter shows you how to work out the essential skills from looking at the university websites for your chosen course. Even if your course is listed, it's definitely still worth going to each university website for the places you're applying to and checking to see if anything is missing. Every course at every university is different - it would be impossible to cover them all in one book.

Skills by course

Finance related courses

- Logical thinking
- Problem solving
- Affinity with numbers

Business and Management related courses

- Problem solving
- Critical thinking
- Creativity
- Ability to see multiple perspectives

Engineering related courses

- Problem solving
- Critical thinking
- Creativity
- Logical thinking

Computer Science

- Logical thinking
- Problem solving
- Affinity with numbers

Medical related courses

- Intellectual curiosity
- Empathy
- Problem solving
- Communication and Relationships

Creative Arts and Design courses

- Creativity

- Problem solving

Biological Sciences

- Critical thinking

- Research

- Intellectual curiosity

Physical Sciences

- Critical thinking

- Research

- Intellectual curiosity

- Affinity with numbers

Law, Politics, International Relations, History

- Critical thinking

- Logical thinking

- Ability to see multiple perspectives

- Research

Geography

- Intellectual curiosity

- Research

- Critical thinking

Finding out what you need to show

What should you do if your course isn't listed above? What should you do even if your course is listed, but you want to write a fantastic Personal Statement tailored to the exact needs of the universities that you're applying to? (Which of course should be everyone reading this book!) This is where you'll need to do a bit of work, research and digging yourself, but thankfully, it isn't difficult. Universities make no secret of what they're looking for in their students, and even the briefest scan of the course webpage should highlight some of the key areas that students will need for success in their course.

Let's assume for example that you've decided that you want to study for a degree in Liberal Arts. UK Liberal Arts degrees come from the American ideas about Liberal Arts Colleges where students study a broad range of subjects and focus on the specific skills that they will need in their future lives. The degree is a fairly new concept for UK universities and students, and there isn't yet a lot of information about it or what you should be emphasising when applying to study it. So how can we find out? The process is simple.

First of all, log onto the course webpage for one of the universities you are planning to apply to and read through all of the information that the university has published to market the course. Almost always, the will be some words, phrases and skills that should be jumping out at you if you've been reading this chapter carefully.

If we look at the BA Liberal Arts site from the University of Leeds (Figure 1.1), you'll notice some familiar words:

Figure 1.1 Leeds University, Liberal Arts BA(Hons)

Clearly and obviously, Leeds are telling us that their students need to show intellectual curiosity. "Interdisciplinary collaborations" is a new skills for us, but is an important addition. Once we've identified some key skill words, make a note of them.

If we dig a little deeper through the course webpage (Figure 1.2), we can start to identify more skills that Leeds are looking for:

"Drawing intuitive connections", essentially another way of saying critical thinking.

"Intellectual skills", refers to our skills such as critical thinking, problem solving, and logical thinking.

"Rhetorical skills", that's communication.

Why study Liberal Arts?

BA Liberal Arts will provide you with:

- In-depth understanding of your major subject and how it relates to other fields.
- The ability to draw intuitive connections between different disciplines.
- Intellectual, practical and rhetorical skills and the ability to apply them to a range of subject areas.
- A diverse and stimulating education that utilises different learning and teaching styles.
- Excellent preparation for the modern workplace, where employers need graduates with a broad skill set.

Figure 1.2 Leeds University Liberal Arts BA (Hons)

Even from just two webpages from one university, we're starting to pull together quite a list of skills that are required by the course that you could write about in your Personal Statement.

To write the best Personal Statement however, you shouldn't just stop at one university, but should continue to visit the websites and read the prospectuses of all the universities you're applying to.

Moving on to look at Keele University's Liberal Arts BA (Figure 1.3), we start to see some skills being repeated, and other skills being added to our list.

Course Overview

Liberal Arts is not like other degrees. Rather than focusing on one academic discipline, a Liberal Arts degree concentrates on the qualities that the student will have when they graduate. It offers a unique opportunity to develop critical and creative skills through study of a wide range of disciplines and approaches. The result is a challenging and engaging programme that contributes to the development of capable, and employable, citizen-graduates.

School link:
Institute of Liberal Arts
and Sciences ➔

Liberal Arts is ideal if you're a creative thinker, enjoy exploring new and varied subjects and want to make a difference to society. Its interdisciplinary approach to some of the world's most pressing problems means you'll study a wide range of subjects, including the social sciences, arts, humanities and natural sciences. Much of the programme is underpinned by innovative teaching. For example, the programme uses a 'living labs' approach, by which field trips engage students with local issues and their potential solutions. Students can pursue hands-on research into Britain's industrial history and current/future-oriented issues of economic regeneration, social challenges and environmental sustainability, citizenship and creativity with opportunities for learning analytical, presentational, writing and research skills.

Figure 1.3 Keele University Liberal Arts BA (Hons)

In the case of Liberal Arts, it's notable that critical thinking comes up again on Keele's website. If a skill is coming up time and time again on every university website that you visit, that shows how important the skill is and that it should definitely be highlighted in your Personal Statement.

From the webpage we can now add creativity to our list, as well as problem solving, referred to by mentioning students who will be engaged in finding "potential solutions".

As you can see, universities do not hide the skills that they are looking for in their students, and the information is freely available on their websites for all to see and read. If you take the time to read their websites and prospectuses carefully, universities are actually quite good at telling you what you should be writing about – it is in their interests after all to help attract the most suitable and qualified students for their degree programmes.

Step 1 Summary - The Importance of Understanding

Knowing what universities want to see in their applicants is essential to writing a successful Personal Statement. Only once you truly understand that can you tailor your application to the course you're applying for. If you know the qualities and skills needed, you can use these as the basis for your Personal Statement to keep it relevant, focused, and successful. Whilst there are the general things that universities are looking for, being able to break down and identify the specific skillsets that you need will give you a huge advantage when you start generating examples, and when you start writing. If you understand your course, you understand how to apply.

It is definitely worth spending time reading the course webpages in detail. From here, you'll be able to pick out the skills that you need to show. Some courses will emphasise critical thinking, others the ability to see multiple perspectives, others will require high levels of creativity, most will require at least basic communication skills. Once you know what is required by your course you'll be able to demonstrate this in your Personal Statement and prove to the university why you're the perfect fit for them.

A Call to Action

Now is the time for you to start researching your course. Either take out your notebook or use Worksheet 1 in Appendix 2 of this book. You can download printable versions of all worksheets at:

www.personalstatementmethod.com

Visit the course pages at each university that you are considering applying to and explore the pages carefully, read slowly. Whenever you see a skill or relevant quality mentioned, take a note of it. If the same skill is coming up for every university, make a note of that too. This will help you to know which skills are most important. After all, you're unlikely to be able to write about all the skills mentioned in your 4000-character statement, so knowing which the highest priority are is also highly useful.

By the time you've finished you'll have a list of skills and qualities to shape your Personal Statement around. Once you have this, you can start to think of examples and ways in which you have demonstrated these skills in your life so far. We'll talk about how to do that in Step 2. For now, put this book down and go and make your skills list.

STEP 2:

ORGANISING YOUR EXPERIENCES

A key phrase that you'll often hear when researching how to write job applications is "don't say it; show it". The same applies to your Personal Statement. It's no good just saying that you have strong critical thinking skills, you need to show where you've demonstrated them. Anyone can say they can do something, to impress an admissions officer you need back yourself up with evidence.

Now that you know the skills you need to show, it's time to come up with examples of where you've demonstrated and developed these skills. It's important that these examples are as specific as possible, and really tied to you. They should reference a specific instance, event, piece of work or activity that you participated in. What you don't want is vague and fluffy examples that could relate to anyone, anywhere, any time. Remember: you're trying to sell yourself and prove how your experiences make you the best and most passionate candidate for your course.

The purpose of this chapter is two-fold. Firstly, it will help you to create a structure in which to organise your examples, which you can later transfer to your statement. Secondly it will guide you in thinking back through your last few years to think of specific examples of things that you've done that match to the skills that the university wants to see. Whilst you could pull your examples from anywhere, it's highly recommended that most examples are also linked to the course and subject you're planning to study. Remember we talked about needing to show a passion for your subject? This is exactly how to do it – don't say that you have a passion, use an organised and deliberate structure to show that you have a passion by giving numerous examples of things that you've done that are relevant.

How to structure your Personal Statement

The more you read about how to write your Personal Statement, the more "methods" you're likely to come across. Some may call it a "Five Paragraph Structure", others may call t an "80/20 Structure", but in essence, they're the same thing. Both methods ask you to pull your examples from specific areas, and both have a focus on using your most course relevant activities in your Personal Statement. Why? Because that's exactly what you should be doing.

These structures are popular quite simply because they work. I know, I know, you're probably quietly protesting right now – you don't want your Personal Statement to come across as formulaic and exactly the same as everyone else's. Don't worry – the structures are just a method of organising. The activities, examples and evidence will still be uniquely yours. More than that, you're reading this book – that means that whilst you're using a similar structure, you're not simply focusing on what you've done and shoehorning it into a generic structure, you're focusing on what skills you've developed and how they make you a perfect fit for the university and the course - you're already a step ahead.

The Five-Paragraph Structure

The "5 Paragraph Structure" does exactly what it says on the tin. It splits your Personal Statement into 5 distinct and different paragraphs, each with a different focus.

Paragraph 1: Why have you chosen this course?

This is your opening paragraph, highlighting your formative interest in the subject and what it is about it that excites you so much that you want to study it at an undergraduate level.

Paragraphs 2, 3 and 4: What have you done that demonstrates your genuine interest in the course?

These paragraphs should bring out examples that are directly relevant to your course or subject. These could be academic examples or super-curricular examples (see below for explanations) but should be clearly evident and directly linked.

Paragraph 5: What you have done outside academics and your conclusion

This is your space for your extra-curricular activities. Your sports, your interests, your musical instruments, your charity work. These do not need to show a direct link but should still show how you've developed relevant skills.

Then, finish with a bang. Conclude your statement in a way that brings completion and helps the admissions officer to remember you.

The 80/20 Structure

The 80/20 Structure doesn't disagree with the 5 Paragraph Structure, it simply assigns percentages to paragraphs based on importance. The 80/20 Structure allocates 80% of your Personal Statement to giving examples from directly relevant activities (paragraphs 1, 2, 3 and 4), and 20% of your statement to your extra-curricular activities and conclusion (paragraph 5). Why? Because UK universities focus on academic matters most.

Remember: admissions officers are looking for passion for the subject, positive attitude towards study, and that candidates can complete their degree. These things come first. As one Recruitment Officer once told me, "If you're applying for History, I want the best Historian. I don't want a second-rate Historian who can play the flute". Subject first always, outside interests that can help you in your course second.

But what an you use for examples?

If we take both of these structures together, that leaves three main areas that you should be able to draw examples from: academic examples, super-curricular examples, and extra-curricular examples. Academic and super-curricular should make up your 80% between them, with extra-curricular taking up only 20%.

What are academic examples?

This is anything that you've done in your lessons that's relevant to your future course. This could be a favourite topic that sparked your interest, a research paper, a group project, or a presentation. Basically, anything that you've done for class or for homework.

What are super-curricular examples?

These are what will make you stand out from other candidates. These are the activities that you've participated in outside of the classroom that are still relevant to your subject. Maybe you read a particularly interesting book related to your course. Maybe you attended lectures, seminars or workshops that are relevant. Maybe you've built websites or robots, participated in a local history project, written a series of poetry or blogs published online. Perhaps you were part of the science club at school. Have you taken part in a Maths or Science Olympiad or been on a tour of the Battlefields of World War One? What about related work experience? All of these are examples that could be used to demonstrate a passion for your subject and a positive attitude towards its study. By participating in events and activities beyond the classroom, you're showing the admissions officer that this is something that you choose to do; you're not forced to do it. You do it because you want to, and you're going to continue exploring and expanding your horizons when you study it at university.

What are extra-curricular examples?

Extra-curricular activities are things that you've done that have absolutely nothing to do with your subject. These can be broad and used to show yourself as a holistic and well-rounded individual. If you're smart however, you'll take it a step further and continue to link this section to relevant skills and attributes. For a first-class Personal Statement, if your extra-curricular activities are going to be worth including, you'll want to link them to the broader soft-skills that will be an asset to you at university.

Played rugby for 5 years? You're probably good at team work and communication. Grade 8 pianist? That's discipline and time management right there. President of the Student Council? Leadership. Participated in charity work? You've likely demonstrated empathy then.

Whilst your extra-curricular activities show your breadth, that doesn't mean you can't also use them to highlight key skills.

Being specific

Making your examples of things you've done as specific as possible is essential. The more detail you can give, the better. Avoid anything that sounds vague or generalised as these tend to sound implausible and will be very difficult to reflect upon when you get to Step 3 and need to show what these examples have taught you or made you think about. For example, if you want to say that you were inspired to study economics by books that you've read, don't just say "books". Name the book. If it was a TED Talk, who was the speaker? What was the title or subject matter of the talk?

Look at the examples – Which are specific? Which are vague and fluffy?

Books:

"Having read a wide range of books about the 2008 economic crisis, I am inspired to study economics because…."

"Vince Cable's book The Storm: The World Economic Crisis and What It Means drew me to the world of economics because it made me think about…."

Competitions:

"During a Mathematics competition that I participated in…."

"When competing in the ASDAN Mathematics Competition"

Projects:

"I am a member of the school's STEM club…"

"As part of an extracurricular project, I was part of a team of 3 who designed and built a scale model of a wooden bridge. We were challenged to minimize the cost of building the bridge whilst still making it stable."

Experiences

"I have always been interested in the First World War…."

"Having visited the Tyne Cot Cemetery in Ypres……"

Hopefully you agree that in all of these pairings, the second example is always more specific. Being specific helps ground your examples in real-world evidence, not hypothetical situations. Being specific helps the admissions officer to picture the situation and gives a sense of realism.

A simple rule of thumb for giving evidence: to be specific, you should always refer to a person, place, date, event or "thing" (bridge building project, Vince Cable's book).

By being as specific as possible with your evidence and ensuring that your examples are relevant to your course, you'll be showing your passion for the subject without ever actually needing to say "I have a passion for Mathematics and Finance". You'll be demonstrating how you've gone beyond what was required of you, and thus, you'll also be showing your positive attitude towards study. This is what admissions officers are looking for, and through giving detailed and specific examples you'll be able to "show it" without ever having to "say it".

Examples of examples and what skills they can show

By now you should be ready to start writing down your own examples of things that you've done and activities you've participated in. If you're still struggling to decide what counts as evidence, this section is designed to give you some "examples of examples" – things that have been written by students that have helped them to write successful Personal Statements. This list is by no means exhaustive, and if you've done something different that's not here, that's great too. This list is simply to give you an idea of the possible things that you could think and make a note of, as well as the skills that they likely highlight. One word of warning: don't just copy these – that won't reflect you, and it won't help you to stand out.

Academic Examples

Research Projects

"For my IB Extended Essay I investigated the efficiency of solar panels, studying the effects of different wavelengths of light on photovoltaic cells."
Subject applied for: Mechanical Engineering
Skills highlighted: Research skills

"I proposed an effective way to shorten students' queuing time to deposit money into the meal card through using Poisson distribution to create a mathematical model."
Subject applied for: Business and Management
Skills highlighted: Problem solving, critical thinking

"Researching a classic and long-debated history topic – the role of nationalism in the causes of the First World War - provided me an excellent opportunity to hone skills like research, analysis, refutation and argumentation"
Subject applied for: English Literature and Creative Writing
Skills highlighted: Critical thinking, the ability to see multiple perspectives

"I researched how the portrayal of search for personal identity by Kambili and Jaja, from "Purple Hibiscus", allude to the political struggles of post-colonial Nigeria."
Subject applied for: International Relations
Skills highlighted: Critical thinking, intellectual curiosity

Module highlights

"For example, when learning about e-commerce, I found out many online companies are using big data. Researching data, I learned that information management is crucial in a company's success. For instance, Apple improves its user experience by analysing its customer feedback."
Subject applied for: Management with Finance
Skills highlighted: Research skills, intellectual curiosity

"During a work attachment I learnt about how stethoscopes can be used to detect bruits which could be due to atherosclerosis. I found this particularly interesting as it was something I had learnt in biology and was keen to apply my theoretical scientific knowledge to the real world. This helped me focus my studies as I was able to make connections and see how what I was learning could be applied in my studies and beyond."

Subject applied for: Medicine
Skills highlighted: Logical thinking, making inter-disciplinary connections

Super-Curricular Examples

Wider reading

"My reading definitely helps me to learn more about this subject, from social psychology by David G. Myers to evolutionary psychology by David M. Buss."

Subject applied for: Psychology
Skills highlighted: Intellectual curiosity

Online courses

"I've also taken an online course in nursing which has helped me learn about the different sectors of healthcare and the different problems of it. One highlight was the importance of triage, and how the medical professionals have to face difficult ethical questions and make tough decisions."

Subject applied for: Medicine
Skills highlighted: Intellectual curiosity, empathy, critical thinking

Work experience

"For my work experience at a factory, I had the chance to participate into the commissioning of a moon cake baking machine, installing the stove and the conveyer belt on the machinery as well as changing the arrangements of the components to set the temperature of the stove."
Subject applied for: Mechanical Engineering
Skills highlighted: Problem solving, logical thinking

Summer schools and conferences

"Attending the Harvard Summit for Youth Leaders in China (HSYLC) gave me my first taste of a Liberal Arts curriculum. I realised that I could not define myself as simply a "science person" or an "arts person" as I was fascinated by courses across various disciplines: from a seminar on Practical Electronics to the History of Hip Hop."
Subject applied for: Arts
Skills highlighted: Self-reflectiveness

Relevant school clubs

"As part of an extracurricular project, I was part of a team of 3 who designed and built a scale model of a wooden bridge. We were challenged to minimize the cost of building the bridge whilst still making it stable."
Subject applied for: Mechanical Engineering
Skills highlighted: Problem solving, logical thinking

Relevant Personal Projects

"I maintained an online presence on a website called Duitang. I incorporated my love for fragrances with my interest in poetry in a project, reviewing a line of perfumes by writing a short poem for each of them, characterising and personifying each scent with a story."

Subject applied for: English Literature and Creative Writing
Skills highlighted: Creativity

Charity work

"MIUI's story inspired me to do my own version of participation marketing. I volunteered for a charity organisation called Shared Love to raise funding for primary school students in rural areas."

Subject applied for: Business
Skills highlighted: Intellectual curiosity

Competitions

"In the "Gamble for Crisis" Business Competition, my skills in business negotiation and problem solving were refined once more. Our team was the tertiary sector in the competition and our goal was to construct the robots and sell them to the government to earn profits."

Subject applied for: Business
Skills highlighted: Problem solving

Extra-Curricular Examples

Sports

"Similarly, as the Captain of the school Rugby team, I have attempted to maximize the opportunities given to our students by reaching out to an external adult team to guide us in our training and provide us with opportunities for competition."
Subject applied for: Music
Skills highlighted: Communication and relationships

Non-relevant Personal Projects

"I have also developed the ability to empathise through a project I founded called "YoloShunde!". "Yoloshunde!" is a micro-blog survival guide to assist foreign expatriates living in my town."
Subject applied for: Liberal Arts
Skills highlighted: Empathy

Student Council

"As a member of the Student Council Executive Committee I have been involved with the organisation of many school events, from leading a group in designing the decor of our school Christmas party to spearheading an investigation into how we could improve the initiative and flexibility of our Student Council members."
Subject applied for: Computer Science
Skills highlighted: Time management and organisation

Travel

"To broaden my international education horizons, I visited a wide range of countries. I spent two weeks in Hwa Chong Institution (Singapore), as well as completing summer schools in the USA and Canada, and participating in a tour of more than 10 UK universities."

Subject applied for: Mathematics and Statistics
Skills highlighted: Participation and engagement, ability to see multiple perspectives

Choir and music

"Being part of the school choir has also given me the opportunity to perform in public and is demonstrative of my outgoing personality."

Subject applied for: Hospitality and Tourism Management
Skills highlighted: Creativity

Participation and Engagement

"Outside of academics, I am a keen follower of fashion and keep up to date with the latest fashion trends which then allows me to anticipate future fashion trends, but even here I notice the similarity in fashion changes to the stock market, and how being able to follow the trend is essential to anticipating its future."

Subject applied for: Finance
Skills highlighted: Intellectual curiosity, critical thinking

These are all real examples of things that students have written in their Personal Statements, all of which were highly successful and received multiple offers from the universities of the students' choosing. You should notice that the best examples are those that are the most specific – the ones that tell you exactly the situation and the student's role in it. What you'll hopefully also notice, is that the students manage to write these in a concise manner – detailed and specific, but short, and without going into a long narrative. Why is this important? Because none of these examples are finished. If you were to stop after giving the example, you'd simply be listing your activities and examples. Whilst giving evidence and examples is important for showing your passion, what comes next is just as important, if not more so. You also need to reflect on your examples and tell the admissions officer what this taught you, what it made you think about, and what you learnt. Welcome to Step 3 – Reflecting on Your Examples.

Step 2 Summary - The importance of organisation, structure and evidence

After this chapter, you should now know how to structure your Personal Statement by splitting it into 5 distinct paragraphs and knowing that you should weight it with at least 80% of your examples directly linked to your chosen course, and at most 20% indirectly linked. This will help you to guarantee that your statement is focused and shows your passion for the subject and positive attitude towards study. Your examples need to be specific and detailed, but also concise and clear. They should cover Academic, Super-Curricular and Extra-

Curricular. You're not giving a narrative of everything you've ever done or telling your life story; you are providing evidence to prove that you're an ideal candidate for the course, for the university, and for future study.

A call to action

Now is the time to put the book down again and take out another piece of paper or refer to Worksheet 2 of Appendix 2 Again, printable version of the worksheets are available at:

www.personalstatementmethod.com

Give yourself three headings of "Academic Examples", "Super-Curricular Examples" and "Extra-Curricular Examples" and write down everything you've done over the past 2 years that fits under each heading. Add the details now, it will make it easier when it comes to writing your Personal Statement. Try to write as many examples as possible, from as many different categories as possible. You can always exclude anything that you decide to be weaker or repetitive later.

Now, put the book down and write out your examples.

STEP 3:

REFLECTIONS

You know what skills you need to show on your application, you know what you've done that's relevant to your course, you're ready to apply. Wait.

You're nearly ready to apply. There's one more step that you're missing that will take your Personal Statement from a mediocre one to a first-class statement that sees the offers flying in. You still need to reflect on your experiences and show what you learnt from each. Being able to reflect with insight, authenticity and individuality is the difference between a Personal Statement that simply lists activities, and a Personal Statement that tells the admissions officer that you are a candidate who is able to engage with your course and excel at your chosen university. If you only have skills and examples in your Personal Statement, you run the risk of the admissions officer assuming that

a)   You did the activities because you thought you had to, not because you wanted to

Or

b)   You may be interested in your course, but you're not capable of engaging with it to a sufficient level where you'll actually be able to complete it.

If we look back at the bridge building example from earlier, which version makes the candidate look more insightful to an admissions officer?

Version 1:

"Recently, as part of an extracurricular project, I was part of a team of 3 who designed and built a scale model of a wooden bridge. We were challenged to minimize the cost of building the bridge whilst still making it stable."

Version 2:

"Recently, as part of an extracurricular project, I was part of a team of 3 who designed and built a scale model of a wooden bridge. We were challenged to minimize the cost of building the bridge whilst still making it stable. This project changed my understanding of real world engineering; previously I had just considered the beauty of the bridge, but now had to consider the realistic factors of cost and stability."

Version 1 gives a solid example of an activity undertaken that would be highly relevant to a Mechanical Engineering application but doesn't necessarily show the student as the driver – "we were challenged" – the task was given by someone else, and without the reflection, we don't know what impact this had on the student.

Version 2 on the other hand, adds just one sentence but raises the statement to a new level by reflecting on how the project changed the mindset of the student and helped her to develop as an Engineer. Suddenly she has gone from the average student, considering only "the beauty of the bridge" to someone who clearly thinks like an Engineer as she takes into account "realistic factors of cost and stability".

In a one sentence reflection, this student has managed to implant the idea in the admissions officer's mind that not only is she interested in Engineering, but she already thinks like an engineer and is able to recognise many of the concerns that Engineers have when working on their projects.

Step 3 demystifies the process of reflection and encourages you to write with authenticity. It will help you to take your examples from their current status of a list of activities and turn them into sections of your Personal Statement that will truly help to highlight your insights and abilities and prove to the admissions officer that you are ready and prepared for university study. The final part of the chapter will then help you to match your activities and reflections to the necessary skills that you identified in Step 1. Once we have successfully matched skills to activities to reflections, then you will have the core of a successful Personal Statement in front of you, and only then will you be ready to start writing it.

What is a reflection anyway?

If we start with the dictionary definition, Oxford Dictionaries call it:

"A serious thought or consideration", elaborating ever so slightly to "An idea about something, especially one that is written down or expressed".

That's probably not Oxford's most helpful definition ever, so we'll need to expand on it if we're going to use it as a guide for Personal Statements. Yes, a reflection is a serious thought or consideration, but it's also more than that. In terms of your Personal Statement, think of your reflections as a way to analyse and examine your examples and activities. Your reflections are your insights into what happened, why they happened, what changed, and what impact they had. To put it simply, your reflections are what you learnt from your activities. This could mean that your reflection is how an event or activity changed your opinion on something or made you think about something else linked and related, or it could be how it taught you a skill or valuable lesson.

If the primary purpose of undergraduate study is learning, then it seems a fair assumption that universities are looking for students who are constantly learning. Learning from things that go right, learning from things that go wrong. Learning knowledge, learning skills, learning how to use knowledge and skills to create new knowledge. This is why your reflections are important, and this is why an authentic and insightful reflection can raise the level of your application significantly.

An example that isn't reflected upon is an example that's wasted. It means you're just making a list and you're not analysing and examining. A reflection doesn't need to be long, often just a sentence or a few lines will do, but it is your reflection that connects your activities to your learning and shows you growing and developing as a student. If nothing else, it is your reflection that makes you sound more interesting and gives the admissions officer a chance to connect with your mind. One common mistake that students make is to cram their Personal Statement full of every tiny thing that they've done over the last two years. A better choice is to select just a few examples that you really connected with, that really impacted upon you, and use your Personal Statement to reflect on these. This will put you at a higher level than someone who has completed 100 related activities and insists on including all of them.

Authenticity and questions to ask yourself

One danger with reflections, is that if you haven't really thought about it, you run the risk of writing what you think the admissions officer wants to hear. What the admissions officer actually wants to hear however, is not a pre-rehearsed and generic thought, but something personal and from you. This is after all a Personal Statement. Reflections that seem too bland and generic won't carry the same weight as someone who takes reflecting upon their own learning seriously and won't have the same level of authenticity. Your reflection is what you learnt, how it impacted you, and what it made you think about. These are not things that can be copied or cribbed, and no one can write these for you. Many students find this the hardest part of their Personal Statement, and as such it's worth spending the most time over in order to really concentrate on it and be able to share something meaningful.

As you read through the examples you've written, the following questions may help to guide you into thinking more reflectively on your experiences:

Overall Experience:

- Are my thoughts about the experience mostly positive or negative? What makes them this way?

- How did this experience impact my thoughts on the subject?

- How did the experience impact those around me?

- How was this experience relevant to the real-world or other areas of my life?

Successes:

- Did I meet my goals? What helped me most in achieving this?

- What strengths can I identify as having helped me to achieve success?

Challenges:

- What was challenging about the experience? What did I find most difficult?

- What did I find hindered progress the most?

- Is there an area that I was weak in that I would be able to improve?

Teamwork and collaboration:

- How well do I feel that I worked with others during this experience?

- What were things that my team mates or I did to help to overcome obstacles?

Learning points:

- What was the most important thing I learnt from this activity?

- If I had to do it again, would I do it the same way or differently? Why?

- After this experience, what's the one thing about myself that I would like to improve?

- How will I use what I've learnt on this experience in the future?

Naturally, not all of these questions will be applicable to all situations, but they're designed for you to use as a starting point to think about your experiences and reflect authentically.

One thing to note is that your examples and reflections don't always have to be positive. It's OK to identify when things didn't quite go right for you, and often this will raise a more meaningful learning point. If everything always goes exactly how we plan it to, then we're perfect and there's nothing to learn right? Being able to identify things that weren't quite right or improvements that you could make shows that you're a reflective learner who's constantly seeking improvement. What's more important than getting everything right, is what you learnt from it, and by extension, what you did next.

"Although my experiment failed at first, redesigning it taught me about the importance of thoroughness and clarity in my thinking processes and the importance of listening to critical feedback in order to improve and succeed."

In this example, the student was able to identify her own weaknesses in the initial experiment's design and recognise clear areas for improvement. This tells an admissions officer far more about a candidate than someone who has apparently always got everything right and apparently never makes mistakes. It tells an admissions officer that the student is able to think for themselves and make improvements.

Turning examples in reflections

So how do we go about turning our examples into reflections? If you ask yourself the Authenticity Questions, the process should be pretty straight forward. Remember that you're looking to examine, analyse and show what you learnt through your experiences, keeping in mind the skills that are relevant for your course.

You can try using the following helpful phrases and sentence starters to link to your examples and emphasise your reflection:

- This taught me that

- This demonstrated my skills in

- This was important because

- It was because of this that I realised

- This changed my opinion about

- This helped me to think more broadly about

- Thinking from this perspective allowed me to

- I discovered that

- This provoked…

- …made me understand

- I found this particularly interesting because

If you can take the example, the answer to one of your authenticity questions, and then add in one of the helpful phrases, you should find that you have a well reflected paragraph forming.

Example from a Marketing Personal Statement:

"I proposed an effective way to shorten students' queuing time to deposit money into the meal card through using Poisson distribution to create a mathematical model."

Authenticity questions and answers:
Question: "What was the most important thing I learnt from this activity?"

Answer: I learnt about the importance of the customer experience to a business

Question: What strengths can I identify as having helped me to achieve success?

Answer: My skills in statistical analysis

Putting it all together:

"I proposed an effective way to shorten students' queuing time to deposit money into the meal card through using Poisson distribution to create a mathematical model. This attempt not only demonstrated my skills in statistical analysis but also helped me to think more broadly about the importance of customer service."

In this part of her Personal Statement, the student was not only able to subtly emphasise her skills in statistical analysis, but also show how an essentially Mathematical problem was making her consider the business and marketing implications of her work; demonstrating both her passion for her chosen course and a level of insight above and beyond her Mathematics project.

Example from a Medicine Personal Statement:

"I explored the best reactants to make aspirin synthesis greener. Experimenting with acetyl chloride, acetic acid and ethanoic anhydride, I was looking to produce a reaction that maximised atom economy as well as see which of the reactants was the safest."

Authenticity questions and answers:

Question: If I had to do it again, would I do it the same way or differently? Why?

Answer: Be more careful when preparing the chemicals - I don't want it to explode again!!!

Putting it all together:

"I explored the best reactants to make aspirin synthesis greener. Experimenting with acetyl chloride, acetic acid and ethanoic anhydride, I was looking to produce a reaction that maximised atom economy as well as see which of the reactants was the safest. Causing a small explosion when I underestimated the reactivity of acetyl chloride taught me to be more cautious and methodical in approaching experiments and chemicals and emphasized the importance of thorough preparation."

This shows that student is reflective enough to admit when he made mistakes, but also that he can identify where he went wrong and seek to further improve himself and his skills in the future: skills admired by all universities.

If you take the time to genuinely work through the authenticity questions on your examples, you should have no trouble producing reflections that are both insightful and sincere. This is what will help most in raising your Personal Statement from one that just lists the activities you completed, to one that shows a university that you have a mind that they want to recruit.

Bringing back your skills list

Examples and reflections, examples and reflections, didn't we start Step 1 by saying we needed to focus on demonstrating the skills that admissions officers were looking for? What you should find, is that from each of your example-reflection notes you should be able to identify a key skill. If you can identify the skill that each example-reflection shows, you'll then be able to align your most essential skills list with your notes on examples and identify which of your examples are the absolute must include, which ones you can include if you've space, and which ones are probably best avoided.

Taking the previous example of using Poisson Distribution to shorten queue times, what skills does this show?

"I proposed an effective way to shorten students' queuing time to deposit money into the meal card through using Poisson distribution to create a mathematical model. This attempt not only demonstrated my skills in statistical analysis but also helped me to think more broadly about the importance of customer service."

This example shows both the student's ability to problem solve, and to think critically. Firstly, she identified the problem that students were facing in long queuing times for their meal cards and looked at how to solve it. Secondly, she was able to apply logic and reasoning from something that she had learnt in her lessons, and then apply it to a new and different situation. In other words, she was thinking critically.

If we take the explosive chemist and his greener aspirin experiment, we should also be able to identify some skills:

"I explored the best reactants to make aspirin synthesis greener. Experimenting with acetyl chloride, acetic acid and ethanoic anhydride, I was looking to produce a reaction that maximised atom economy as well as see which of the reactants was the safest. Causing a small explosion when I underestimated the reactivity of acetyl chloride, this taught me to be more cautious and methodical in approaching experiments and chemicals and emphasized the importance of thorough preparation."

Clearly, he's implying his research skills by making reference to the experiments he's completed in the past, but he's also demonstrating that he's a reflective learner who can identify where he went wrong and how this helped him to improve in future research.

Matching your examples and reflections to specific skills will help you to know which should receive most time and emphasis in your Personal Statement. How you choose to handle them from here is then up to you. You could make direct reference to the skills developed in your paragraph, or you could leave them to be inferred by the admissions officer. The Poisson Distributor for example chose to start her paragraph by directly stating she had developed critical thinking skills and then giving the example above. The explosive chemist on the other hand chose to leave his research and reflectiveness to inference and use his example to highlight his intellectual curiosity, another skill he had identified that is demonstrated in his example.

Step 3 Summary - The importance of reflections

Reflections are what take you from an average Personal Statement, to one that stands out at a level above the majority. Your reflections are the part of your Personal Statement that show you to be mature enough for advanced studies. They show you to be constantly learning and seeking improvement. They show that you have the inquisitiveness, insightfulness, and the abilities to not just survive, but to excel in your future university and course.

If you can match your examples, to your reflections, to the skills you have, to the skills desired by your future university course, you have the makings of a very strong and effective Personal Statement. Coming up with your skills, examples and reflections is the difficult bit. If you can do this successfully, the process of actually writing the Personal Statement is simple and straightforward.

A call to action

At the end of this chapter you now have two tasks:

First, you need to sit down with each of the examples you identified previously and start to make reflective notes. You can use the authenticity questions from this chapter to help you. This is how you turn your examples from just a list of things, into something you can use in your Personal Statement.

Second, you need to match each of these example-reflection pairings to different skills. If you can correctly identify the skills that you've been displaying, you'll know which examples you need to use, and which ones are less important to you.

Again, Worksheet 3 is available in Appendix 2 to help you.

So, once more, book down, reflection time.

STEP 4:

WRITING THE STATEMENT

Finally, it's time to start putting words onto the page and start crafting your Personal Statement. You know what skills you need to show, you know what examples of experiences you're going to use to show them, and you know exactly what each of these experiences taught you. You know your overall structure. It's time to start putting that all together and turning it into your masterpiece.

One thing that you want to make sure of when writing is that your Personal Statement stands out in the mind of the admissions officer - after all, he or she could be reading thousands of these. This means that you need to think carefully about how you open your statement with a winning introduction, as well as how you close it with a memorable finish. It means you need to avoid the same over-used words and phrases that come up time and time again, and you need to focus on making yourself the centre of your statement. It also means you need to consider the structure of each paragraph in order to keep it concise and focused on bringing out your skills, passion and ideas.

That is what we're going to look at in this chapter:

- What makes a good introduction?

- What words, phrases and clichés should you avoid?

- How can you use active language to ensure that you remain the protagonist of your statement?

- How should you structure each paragraph and how do you use the PEEL format?

- How can you use your closing statements to sum up your experiences and answer any final questions that the admissions officer may have about you?

- What are some final things that you should do, and things that you definitely shouldn't do when writing the statement?

By the time you've finished with this chapter you'll be ready to complete your first draft. Everything else should now be in place and your preparation should be over: it's time to get down to actually writing your Personal Statement.

Introducing your statement

The introduction is the first thing your admissions officer will read in your Personal Statement. From here they'll form their first impression and first impressions count. You may hear it said that if they don't like your introduction they won't read the rest of the statement; whilst I've never heard of that actually being the case, your introduction does have the power to make your admissions officer read your statement with a smile or with a frown, so it's generally best to start on a positive note. That said, don't go overboard. You should avoid sounding gimmicky, clichéd or over the top. Sounding too contrived can put an admissions officer off more than anything else, so what should you actually do?

- Be yourself
- Show your enthusiasm
- Get to the point
- End with the start

Being yourself

There is no need to try to paint yourself as the world's deepest thinker and a philosopher in the making (I'm just assuming that's not you). You're far better to write what comes naturally and from yourself. One thing that this means is that you should avoid quotes. Some students like to use them as a starting point to link to their own ideas; other students like to throw them in to "look clever and well-read" but then never actually refer to them again. A quote shows the thoughts of others, not yourself, and so should generally be avoided. Wasting 200 characters of your precious 4000 on the thoughts of others is nothing but a waste and is often cited as a "pet hate" of admissions officers. Instead, you'd be better to explain what it is that made you interested in the course, how the course will benefit you, and just what it is that excites you about your future study path.

Showing your enthusiasm

One thing you can use your introduction for is to show the admissions officer what it first was that drew you to your chosen course, or if not what was the first thing, an example of something impactful that you did that made you realise that this was the best course and option for you. One way to do this is to jump straight in with an example. Was there one specific experience that kickstarted your interest? Or was it a series of smaller events happening over time?

Starting with an example has the advantages of being linked directly to you, showing where your enthusiasm came from, and getting straight to the point. Again though, avoid being totally over the top. If you're trying to tell the admissions officer that you used to wake up as a 5-year-old after an exciting dream about the thrills of actuary, they'll know you're either lying, or a complete weirdo. Some students worry about this section as they haven't "always known" what they wanted to do. This could be an advantage rather than a disadvantage - there's no need to bore the admissions officer with what inspired you when you were little. If it's inspiring you now, that's enough, lead with that.

Getting to the point

Avoid waffle; avoid long, drawn out narratives of what first interested you in your course; avoid beating around the bush and instead jump straight in with getting to the point as quickly and specifically as possible. The best Personal Statements will show the admissions officer right from line one that this is a course you are passionate about and suitable for without needing the admissions officer to make inferences or wade through lines of drivel to understand what you're getting at. A Personal Statement isn't the place to build suspense and stun your reader with a shocking twist at the end. Focused, to the point, specific. Start that way and keep that flowing.

Ending with the start

Although your introduction comes at the beginning, you don't need to write it first. Many people find that it's easier to write their body paragraphs first, and then come back to their introduction at the end. This way you already know exactly where your statement is leading and can ensure that your introduction properly sets the tone and flow for what's to come.

Examples of introductions:

Engineering:

"Scientists discover the world that exists; engineers create the world that never was. It is this application of science to the world that excites me so much about engineering; from daily life applications such as how watches work, to amazing feats of human engineering like aeroplanes and skyscrapers. Recently, as part of an extracurricular project, I was part of a team of 3 who designed and built a scale model of a wooden bridge…." (You know where this example is going, you've seen it before!)

English and Creative Writing:

"English, albeit a foreign language, has always held a great fascination for me. Unlike many of my contemporaries who find English learning tedious and demanding, I read English books for pleasure. The exquisite vocabulary of English and especially how writers use it to depict real or imaginary worlds and plot stories mesmerises me profoundly. Throughout the years of being a diligent literature reader, I came to understand the power of language. Therefore, I wish to learn how to wield the magic of language myself, hoping one day I can build a world of my own using paper and ink, in which people can find beauty, quietude and comfort just as I have in others'. Also, from people like Khaled Hosseini and Lu Xun who have woven politics and humanitarian causes into literature, I discovered that literature can actually make an impact on society in its own poetic way. Therefore, I want to turn my interest in English language and my skill of writing into something more meaningful, and that requires further study in my higher education."

International Relations:

"After 12 years in Singapore, the country my sister and I grew up in, and our family called home, we had to leave because our respective visas would not be renewed. Consequently, we were faced with forceful deportation in a months' time, and I was prevented from completing my GCE 'O' Level. This experience inspires me to ensure that youths all over the world never worry about having an education because of the passport they hold, nor are disadvantaged by narrow-minded policies of domestic politics."

Business and Marketing:

"Winning the championship in the "Gamble for Crisis" Business Competition helped to develop my interest in exploring the world of business in depth and motivated me to complete a rewarding internship at Hisense in 2017. During this practice, I was able to participate in the operation of some of the core business by virtue of my solid basis in business knowledge, which deepened my understanding of the significance of effective business strategies in maintaining enterprises' sustainable development. Therefore, I aspire to turn myself into a business talent with an international horizon."

Avoiding overused words and clichés

When words are used too often, they lose their meaning. When admissions officers see a word too often, it makes them think negatively of the statement and the candidate. Through knowing which words and phrases admissions officers see too much of, you'll be able to avoid falling into this trap. Similarly, many candidates revert to clichés in their writing, largely because they have become such a normal part of everyday speech. Generally, though, your admissions officer will ignore them, and they lack the power to engage the reader.

Overused words

Throughout this book, and no doubt from everything else you've been told and read, you've been reminded that you need to show your passion in your Personal Statement.

The most overused word in a Personal Statement then?

"Passion"

The word "passion" comes up in more Personal Statements than almost any other and should be avoided. You need to show your passion, not say that you have passion.

Phrases such as:

- "I have a passion for..."

- "I am passionate about..."

- "My passion for...led me to..."

should generally be avoided.

Other words that are overused and should be avoided include:

- "Fascinating" - don't tell me it was fascinating. Fascinate me. Show me why it's fascinating.

- "Good/interesting" - these words have little meaning. There are far better ways of showing something to be good or interesting than using these words.

Overused phrases and clichés

In 2015, UCAS surveyed the most commonly used phrases in Personal Statements, particularly in the opening lines. At all costs, avoid opening your statement with one of these phrases:

- "From a young age I have always been interested in..." (seen 1,779 times in 2015)

- "For as long as I can remember I have..." (seen 1,451 times in 2015)

- "I am applying to this course because…" (seen 1,370 times in 2015)

- "I have always been interested in…" (seen 927 times in 2015)

- "Throughout my life I have always enjoyed…" (seen 310 times in 2015)

These phrases have been used so often, that they're too unoriginal. If these phrases appear in your Personal Statement they are likely to instantly turn off the admissions officer.

Other things that come up often include:

- Engineers talking about LEGO - seemingly, LEGO has been responsible for creating more Engineers than anything else.

- Doctors wanting to help people - there's nothing wrong with wanting to help people, but it doesn't make an interesting Personal Statement.

- Doctors talking about someone in their family with a terrible disease - I'm surprised that medics can get out of bed in the morning, so many of them seem to come from backgrounds marred by medical tragedies.

- Fire related metaphors - "sparked", "ignited", "burning desire" - I have no idea why these come up so often, but they do.

- Chemists setting fire to themselves with their junior chemistry set - clearly better safety instructions are needed here, they seem to be a death trap.

All of these come over as false, and the frequency with which they seem to happen tells admissions officers that they can't all be true. You don't need an amazing stand-out moment that inspired you, stick to the truth and you'll come across far better, far more sincere, far more authentic.

Active language

Using "active" language, or the "active voice", instead of "passive" language will make your Personal Statement more direct, more concise, and more engaging for the reader. It can make your text stronger and show responsibility for actions, as well as being generally shorter than the passive form.

Active language is a sentence where it is clear that the subject of the sentence performs the action. Passive on the other hand, is when the subject has the action done to it.

Example:

Passive: In the summer of 2016 I was given the opportunity to participate in an internship at the Bank of China.

Active: In the summer of 2016 I participated in an internship at the Bank of China.

Here, the active form has two distinct advantages for a Personal Statement:

The active form gives the student more credit for the internship - they were the one who completed it. In the passive, although it does say that the student completed the internship, the sentence structure gives more credit to the one who provided the opportunity.

It is more than 25% shorter. The passive form needed 103 characters to form the sentence, the active only 75. When you only have 4,000 characters to play with, can you really afford to waste it on giving credit to other people?

How do you use active language?

- Identify the subject of your sentence - who or what is the sentence really talking about? Who is performing the action?

- Identify the direct object - what is being acted upon?

- Identify the verb - what is the action being taken?

- Make sure that the subject is the one doing the action to something else.

Example:

In the summer of 2016 I [subject] participated [verb] in an internship [direct object] at the Bank of China.

Example:

Passive: In the business competition my skills in business negotiation and problem solving were refined once more.

The subject of this sentence should be the student. The object should be her skills. The verb is "refining" her skills.

Active: In the business competition I refined my skills in business negotiation and problem solving.

To think of it more simply, if you've written a sentence that includes "to be + past participle" (was or were + past participle), it's probably in the passive voice and you should try to reword it into the active voice.

Paragraphing

Paragraphs form the basis of your Personal Statement and the usual writing conventions apply. To ensure that your statement is organised and easy to read it's important to stick to the basic rule of paragraphs: one idea, one paragraph. This will usually mean that every skill or example you want to write about will deserve its own paragraph. This helps the reader, in this case the admissions officer, to read your statement with ease, as well as signifying new steps in the development of your statement.

In almost all writing your paragraphs should begin with a topic sentence: what is the paragraph about? This should then be followed by a few sentences in which you give examples and explain the point in hand, followed by a final sentence that either emphasises the point, gives an important consequence, or links through to the next point of the statement.

An easy way to do this is to follow the PEEL structure:

P: Point - your topic sentence, the main thing you're going to talk about in the paragraph

E: Example - What evidence do you have for this? This is where you give the details of what you did, and the activities you participated in.

E: Explain - Why is this important? Why should the reader by interested in this? For your Personal Statement, this will most often be your reflection and a demonstration of what you learnt through this example.

L: Link - How does this make you a strong candidate for the course? What were the consequences of this? What developments stem from here?

Using the PEEL structure will force you to keep your paragraphs focused and concise, but at the same time include all of the important information that your admissions officer needs to see.

Consider the following example:

P: I have made inter-disciplinary connections throughout my IBDP study.

E: For example, for my Extended Essay I chose to explore the relationship between Chemistry and Art. When assisting toning colours for art, I was constantly distracted by the acrid smell of dye and was aware that synthetic dye can be toxic to the human body. I decided to use my knowledge of Organic Chemistry to compare the characteristics of azo and natural dye, aiming to improve methods of producing natural dye.

E: During this exploration I was fascinated by the way that the abstract chemical formula of diazonium salts on paper could transfer into a vivid indigo dye after coupling with phenol.

L: From this investigation, what I have learnt is far beyond Chemistry knowledge itself, but more about how to conduct interdisciplinary research. I learnt how to investigate the relationship between two subjects using scientific methods.

Point: In this example it is clear from the beginning what the student wants to talk about: her abilities to make inter-disciplinary connections.

Example: She then gives the example of her IBDP Extended Essay, giving enough detail to explain to the admissions officer what she did, without turning it into a long narrative that simply describes.

Explain: By talking about the aspect that interested her most, she is giving the admissions officer insights into the way she thinks and the kind of connections that she is able to make.

Link: To conclude the paragraph she emphasises the skills learnt and the focus on inter-disciplinary skills without being repetitive, highlighting that although she was learning Chemistry, her biggest take-away was how the skills she used were transferable and could be used to bridge different disciplines.

Other notes about paragraphs

To assist the flow of the statement, it is often useful to show the relation to the previous paragraphs at the start of the topic sentence, especially if the ideas are linked. Helpful phrases to do this include:

- Again
- Similarly
- For the same reason

Avoid ending a paragraph with unimportant details or digressions. It is important that your final sentence in each paragraph appropriately concludes the point by being relevant and grounding the paragraph within the context of your Personal Statement.

The memorable finish

Just as your opening sentences should set the tone of your statement and make it stand out to the admissions officer, your closing paragraph is your opportunity to end with a bang and truly convince them to put you into the "offers" pile.

If you're following the 5 Paragraph Structure, your closing paragraph is the place to include your extra-curricular activities that you believe make you stand out from other candidates. Do remember though to link them to the skills and attributes that will help you to be a success at university. There's little point in writing about your rugby successes without a reference to your teamwork skills; little to be gained from emphasising your leadership roles without explaining what you gained from them; and no reason for just listing all of your activities without explaining why they're important and relevant.

International students may also want to use the closing paragraph to highlight how they can assure the admissions officer that they're a good fit for studying in the UK. There's no need to mention your amazing IELTS results, they can see these elsewhere, but if you've spent time overseas or visited the universities you're applying to, this is good for the admissions officer to know as it helps them to be sure that you're not just blindly following rankings and that your choices are thorough and well thought out.

Some universities, although not all, appreciate hearing about what your plans for the future are. If you've a specific goal in mind for what you'll do after completing the course, this is the place to put it. Try to be clear and specific about which aspects of the course will help you most in achieving this goal. Again, this is a way to show thorough research and that you know what you're applying for. Be careful however that the aspect you choose is present on all 5 of the courses you're applying for: if it's not part of one of the courses, this tactic could backfire and show that you haven't in fact done thorough research.

Examples of closing paragraphs:

Business:

"I am a member of a public speaking club, a drama club and an art club. Packed with assignments and tasks both from the school and clubs, these areas of learning helped me to have a more creative mind, yet at the same time become more disciplined. For instance, having to manage so many tasks concurrently has helped me to become more efficient and to use my time more effectively. As the Vice-President of the Art Club, I found that I was able to guide my juniors in developing these skills also, sharing my ideas and experiences. Having studied in an International Education Institution, with many Overseas Education Programmes, including the UK, I am confident in my abilities to adapt to the new environment that studying overseas will bring, and look forward to continue to pursue business management academically."

Engineering:

"Having visited several UK university Open Days in the summer of 2016 I am confident that I can adapt to life in the United Kingdom. I am a confident and outspoken person, and have won prizes for my debating skills, as well as reaching the semi-finals of a city-wide public speaking competition. Debate improves my research skills and shows that I am a good communicator and thinker. I have also participated in a wide range of activities outside of normal school life, including developing teamwork through my volleyball team, learning about financial and time management through the organisation of a "Business Bazaar" and whole school "Games Day", and reflecting on my experiences of volunteering once a month at a local autism centre. Studying piano for ten years has taught me about the value of discipline in practising and frequent overseas travel has made me a more open-minded and well-rounded person, who is ready for the challenge of university education in the UK."

Mathematics and Statistics:

"To broaden my international education horizons, I visited a wide range of countries. I spent two weeks in Hwa Chong Institution (Singapore), as well as completing summer schools in the USA and Canada, and participating in a tour of more than 10 UK universities. These experiences introduced me to people with diverse cultural backgrounds, making me more open-minded. Furthermore, I became more self-motivated since international education gives more flexibility to students, which is something that inspires me to continue to study internationally in the future."

Dos and don'ts

When writing your Personal Statement, there are some things that you should do, and others that you certainly shouldn't. Some of these may seem obvious, and others not so, but they're all important to keep in mind when you're writing.

Do:

Be specific - as mentioned in Step 2, it's important that you're as specific as possible, and your examples should reflect this. If you've followed the guidance in Step 2, this shouldn't be a problem for you.

Be enthusiastic - remember you're trying to show your passion for the course and for your future studies. This is something that you're planning to spend the next 3 to 4 years of your life doing, and you should be enthusiastic about it. This is not the place to be cautious and modest, your enthusiasm should be evident throughout.

Use your own voice - this is a Personal Statement, it should come from you, in your own voice. Some students try to sound very "academic" in their Personal Statement, but this often leads to a statement that is very dry to read, tends to lack clarity, and doesn't represent the student in their best light.

Organise your statement - this one shouldn't need saying if you've been reading carefully so far. Organisation makes your statement easy to read and highlights the key points. Refer to Step 2 for guidance on how to structure your statement and remember to use clear and concise paragraphs.

Don't:

Plagiarise - it's OK to look at examples of successful Personal Statements, it's not OK to copy them. For a start, you're likely to get caught as UCAS uses plagiarism detection software. More than that, the experiences and skills in other peoples' Personal Statements are not your own and so your statement is likely to come across as false.

Try to use humour - it's just not worth the risk. The admissions officer may not have the same sense of humour as you. At worst you risk offending them, at best you'll likely sound like you lack seriousness and dedication or are too flippant. Save humour for your friends; admissions officers are serious people.

Lie or over-exaggerate - don't make up experiences you haven't had; you may be asked to provide evidence or asked about them at interviews. Don't overstate your abilities or experiences either; no one is expecting ground-breaking research or broken world records. It's easy for admissions officers to tell if you're potentially overstating the truth, and it casts doubt on your other achievements too. Be open and honest (but positive!).

Simply describe your experiences - remember, it's not a list of everything you've ever done. It's far more important to reflect on your experiences and tell the admissions officer what you learnt.

Talk about your grades - there's a place for your grades on the UCAS form, you don't need to repeat the information in your Personal Statement. The admissions officer will be able to see all of this together, and you haven't space for repeated information. Even if there's a particular and valid reason why your grades were lower than they should have been, the Personal Statement isn't the place to give that reason. Your reference writer should include this in their reference, so do speak to them if you're in doubt.

Refer to any university specifically - you're sending an identical Personal Statement to 5 universities. Nottingham might not be too impressed if you dedicate a section of your Personal Statement to writing about how impressed you are by Imperial and how you're definitely the best student for them. Focus on the course and subject, not the universities.

Waste space with irrelevant information - apply the "so what?" rule to every point, paragraph and example. Your ability to eat 100 doughnuts in 10 minutes might be impressive, but unless you can show how it makes you a good candidate for the course, it's not relevant in your Personal Statement.

Try to use big words - admissions officers are rarely impressed by them. They make your statement harder to read, and if used wrongly can make your meaning unclear. Stick to simple, clear and direct language.

Make unsupported claims - don't tell universities that you're "the best applicant ever" or "the world's greatest mathematician". If you can't back it up, don't say it.

Step 4 Summary – The Importance of Good Writing

You should now be ready to start writing your Personal Statement. You should have some ideas about how to keep your reader engaged with powerful opening and closing sentences, and you should know what phrases to avoid due to their overuse. Remember that it's important to show your best self, and not fall into the trap of trying to say what you think the admissions officers want to hear. Trying to use quotes to sound clever, or over-exaggerating your skills and experiences will ring hollow with admissions officers and not present you in the way you intend.

Using the PEEL structure for your paragraphs and active language for your examples will help to keep your Personal Statement focused, concise and with you at the centre. You should know the kind of general and easy to avoid errors that turn admissions officers off. Keep a close eye on the "dos" and "don'ts" and you shouldn't go far wrong.

A call to action

This is it! Pen to paper, fingers to keyboard. Now is the time to finally start writing one of the most important documents of your life so far. Set aside a couple of hours, get yourself a nice hot cup of tea, and lock yourself away somewhere where you won't be disturbed. Gather up all of your notes from the previous few chapters and then turn off your phone and the internet. You don't need them anymore for looking up tips and tricks on how to write; you already have everything you need. From here on in, the internet will be nothing but a wonderful source of distraction.

Remember that you don't have to write your Personal Statement in order. If you're struggling with one section or paragraph, feel free to leave it for now and come back to it later. Similarly, this is not the time to strive for perfection. You'll want to edit and redraft your statement once it's finished anyway. So, for now, concentrate on getting words onto the page. We'll look at editing and polishing it in the next chapter.

So, book down, writing time.

STEP 5:

EDITING THE STATEMENT

Your first draft is done! Before you move on to editing it's best to give yourself some time so that you can come back and re-look at your Personal Statement with fresh eyes. In an ideal world you'll be able to leave it alone for at least a week. In a less ideal world, try and give it a few days. If you've left it to the last minute, a few hours are still absolutely mandatory. Walking away from your statement and coming back later will help you to spot errors and inconsistencies that you perhaps didn't see after spending hours reading and rereading what you've written.

A thorough and careful editing process will ensure that your Personal Statement is sent free of typos, spelling, and grammar mistakes. It will help you to make sure that your statement says exactly what you meant it to say, and that this is clear and easily understood by others. Editing will also help you to avoid slipping into monotony, as well as ensuring that you keep the word count under control to bring your statement down to within the stipulated 4000 characters.

Those are the key areas that we're going to look at in this chapter:

- Avoiding spelling and grammar mistakes

- Key grammar and style points that sometimes get missed

- Avoiding the over use of "I" when starting sentences about yourself

- Bringing the word count under control

- Getting your Personal Statement checked by somebody else.

By the end of this chapter, your Personal Statement should be complete, packaged, polished and ready to upload to the UCAS website. This is it. The final step on your Personal Statement journey.

Spelling and grammar

You must demonstrate correct spelling and grammar. Few things are more off-putting to an admissions officer than a Personal Statement strewn with spelling and grammar mistakes. It makes it harder to read, it has the potential to confuse your reader and it shows a lack of care, attention to detail and proofreading. This applies not only to UK students, but to international student applications also. When asked how important it was for international students to eradicate all of their grammar mistakes in their Personal Statement, bearing in mind that they are usually writing in their second language, Leeds University once told me "This is probably one of the most important documents they've ever written, we expect them to be able to take the time and put the thought into it to fix the errors". No allowances are made, spelling and grammar are important for all students. Unfortunately, mistakes are also extremely easy for admissions officers to spot, and often jump out from the page, distracting from otherwise excellent content.

How can you avoid spelling and grammar mistakes? The first and most obvious answer, is to do the first draft of your statement in word processing software such as Microsoft Word, Pages, or OpenOffice. These will help to identify your most glaring typos and errors by underlining them in red and green. Is this enough? Definitely not. Helpful as word processing spell checking tools are, they are not enough to remove errors from writing. A spell checker fails when you mistype the word you meant, and instead type something that is still a word.

"I was keen to explore the role of the pheasants in the French Revolution of 1789."

As interesting a topic as revolutionary pheasants may be, it is unlikely that this is what the candidate meant. More likely they were aiming to write "peasants". This kind of error will never be picked up by a word processor but will definitely be picked up by an admissions officer (and in this case, probably passed around the admissions office for everyone to have a good laugh at, but not in a good way for you). Similarly, your software is unlikely to be able to distinguish between such common errors as confusing "to", "too" and "two", or "there" and "their".

Relying on software alone is not enough, so what else can you do? Repeated re-reading of your statement specifically looking for spelling and grammar errors is essential, however, after you've already spent so much time on it it's likely that your brain will gloss over mistakes if you attempt to re-read it straight away. If you have the time before the UCAS deadline, set your statement aside for a few days and come back to it with fresh eyes. You'll almost certainly notice mistakes that you missed last time.

Finally, if spelling and grammar mistakes jump out at admissions officers, they're also likely to jump out at other readers of your statement too. There is nothing wrong with giving your statement to others to get them to help you to identify mistakes, and indeed it is recommended. Show your statement to your parents or teachers, or anyone else who you believe to have strong spelling and grammar. Ask them to specifically look out for mistakes. It may even be helpful to give them questions to answer when reading it:

- Can you see any spelling or grammar mistakes?

- Can you identify where I've written one word but you suspect I meant another?

- Are my tenses consistent throughout my statement?

- Is there anywhere you are not clear about what I mean?

Ask them to read it at least twice, looking for nothing other than spelling and grammar mistakes, and you should be able to produce a statement that is free from basic and obvious errors.

A quick grammar and style lesson

Please don't skip this section! Whilst I'm sure that this is going to feel a little bit like stepping back into an English lesson, there are certain grammar and stylistic mistakes made all too commonly that you should pay close attention to when crafting your statement.

The use of apostrophes

Apostrophes have two uses. To show possession, and to shorten compound words. You do not need them before every "s"!

Singular Possession: Where something belongs to something else, and that something else is singular (only one thing). The apostrophe comes before the "s".

Example 1: "My team's victory in the Model United Nations competition…"

Victory here belongs to the team, and there is only one team.

Example 2: "I was inspired by my Chemistry teacher's words"

The words belong to the Chemistry teacher, and there is only one Chemistry teacher.

Plural possession: Where something belongs to something else, but that something else is plural (more than one).

The apostrophe comes after the "s".

Example 1: "The teams' skills contributed to their performance"

The skills belong to the teams, and there is more than one team.

Example 2: "I was inspired by my teachers' words"

The words still belong to the teachers, but this time there was more than one teacher.

Word contractions: Used in words such as "don't" or "won't", where you're shortening the full forms of "do not" and "will not". As this usage of the apostrophe is generally quite informal language, it's best avoided in your Personal Statement.

Semi-colons

Some people use semi-colons whenever they're not sure what other punctuation to use. In your Personal Statement, they should only have two uses: to link and to separate.

1. To link two related clauses that could otherwise by joined by a conjunction (but, and, however, because) or separated by a full stop.

"I enjoy studying Philosophy. It helps me to think logically."

"I enjoy studying Philosophy because it helps me to think logically."

"I enjoy studying Philosophy; it helps me to think logically."

Note: The clauses must be related to each other. "I enjoy studying Philosophy; French helps me to understand other people." would not be acceptable.

2. To separate items on a complex list (a list in which the items are long and have their own punctuation such as commas).

"From my work experience I learnt how to manage my time and deadlines; work with other, external, stakeholders; and gained an insight into the inner workings of the industry."

Note: This usage should probably be avoided in a Personal Statement, as listing is something that we're aiming to avoid.

Colons

Again, colons are often used where they shouldn't be. The three main uses include: a definition or expansion of an initial statement, to set up a quotation, to introduce a list.

1. Definition or expansion of an initial statement.

"Chemistry has made me think more deeply: it has led me to question the building blocks of the universe and how the world came to be."

2. To set up a quotation.

"My teacher often told me: "As one pursuing knowledge, you must be a risk taker.""

3. To introduce a list.

"My work experience taught me the following skills: time management, communication, empathy."

Note: Again, avoid this usage; it's just listing!

Avoiding "I"

If you're writing about yourself, it's perfectly normal to write "I" a lot. If you start every sentence or paragraph with "I" however, this quickly becomes monotonous to the reader and makes it boring to read.

- "I am deeply intrigued by the world of biology"
- "I participated in a research project about stem cells"
- "I completed work experience at…"
- "I am a member of several clubs and societies"

Whilst there is nothing technically wrong with this, it will make your Personal Statement stilted and you'd be better to infuse some variety to your sentence structure.

Consider using "I" halfway through the sentence to change your sentence structures and make your Personal Statement a more enjoyable read.

- "Deeply intrigued by the world of biology, I…"

- "Having participated in a research project about stem cells, I…"

- "When I completed my work experience at a machine manufacturing plant I…"

- "As a member of several clubs and societies I…"

As well as reducing the monotony of beginning all sentences with "I", placing your "I" in the middle of the sentence has the added benefit of allowing you to develop and expand upon the initial statement without needing to start a new sentence. This will help to make your writing more concise and encourage you to include specific details and reflections in your sentences.

Reducing the wordcount

With all of your skills, experiences and reflections written out, you may come to the point where you find that you've written too much. Remember that you only have 4000 characters, including spaces, to use when entering your Personal Statement onto the UCAS form. You'll need to edit your Personal Statement down to this length, and this is the time to be almost cruel with your words, cutting and killing anything that is irrelevant, unnecessary, or simply too wordy.

Focus on the most relevant

All the way back in Step 1 you made a list of the skills that were relevant for the application to your course and highlighted the ones that came up most often in university websites. These were the skills that were most important. Once you've identified the most important, you may want to consider giving less space to those which you deem less important.

Similarly, whilst you may have dedicated much of your last few years to various extra-curricular activities and they may be incredibly personally important to you, if your links to how they will prepare you for your future studies are tenuous at best, you should look at how you can shorten or even remove this section.

Avoid unnecessary adjectives, adverbs and descriptions

Your Personal Statement is not a work of high literature, and flowery language generally does not benefit your application. Admissions officers are not looking for delicate prose and elaborate penmanship (unless you're applying for a Creative Writing course), and the inclusion of multiple adjectives and adverbs can indeed make your statement more descriptive than reflective. It's better to include more convincing and persuasive content than fluff up your statement with words used only for setting a scene.

"When assisting toning colours for art, I was *constantly* distracted by the *dry, acrid* and *stale* smell of dye, and was aware that *synthetic* dye can be toxic to the *human* body."

In this example, the adjectives and adverbs are highlighted by italics. To what extent do they add to the student's description? If we remove them, does it take anything away from the message? In this example, the adjective synthetic is essential as it shows that the student was focusing on synthetic dyes rather than natural, but the others add little weight.

"When assisting toning colours for art, I was distracted by the smell of dye, and was aware that synthetic dye can be toxic to the body."

Removing the words "constantly" "dry, acrid and stale" as well as "human" takes nothing away from the message or meaning but saves 43 characters. That's more than 1% of the total Personal Statement character count that could have been used up in one sentence without adding value.

Go through your Personal Statement and assess each of your adjectives and adverbs - is it essential, or is it fluff? Cutting unnecessary descriptors is a good way to bring your character count under control, whilst at the same time making your writing more concise and less narrative.

A couple of side notes

For reasons known only to the programmers at Microsoft and the website developers at UCAS, there appears to be a slight discrepancy in the way they count characters: it is not uncommon for Microsoft Word to report your character count at 4000, but when you copy it to UCAS it still says it's too long. Usually the discrepancy is around 4 characters, sometimes up to 10. This is not a huge deal, but it is something to bear in mind when you're editing in your word processing software. Therefore, it's generally best to try and edit your statement down to around 3990 characters. This should mean you don't need to edit it again once you copy it over.

A second issue that causes stress and fear when copying your statement over to UCAS, is that as well as the 4000-character limit, there's also a 47-line limit. What this means is that those of us who've been educated to leave a blank line between paragraphs often get confused when we meet a UCAS form. Don't worry about this, just go ahead and delete the blank line (although still start each paragraph on a new line!). Admissions officers are aware of the limits and know that it's not your fault. No candidate in the history of the world has ever been denied admission to university for not leaving a blank line between paragraphs.

Getting it checked

Once you've got your Personal Statement into a state where you think it's complete, it's time to get someone you trust to cast their eyes over it too. A fresh pair of eyes can often help in spotting errors that you've missed after hours of pouring over it or can highlight areas where perhaps you're not being as clear as you thought you were. You might know exactly what you're talking about, but someone else may be able to point out where more clarifications are needed.

As mentioned in the spelling and grammar section, it's helpful to give specific questions when asking someone to look over your statement for language errors. Similarly, if they're looking for content errors or inconsistencies, then a set of questions can also help to guide them:

- Are there any examples that you don't think truly express the point I was trying to make?

- Are there any examples that aren't fully explained in terms of what I learnt?

- Would you say that it shows my passion for the course I'm applying to?

- Do you think that it is completely focused on the course?

- Is there anywhere where it gives too much information?

- Is that anywhere that you need more information to understand what I'm saying?

- Does it interest you enough to want to read to the end, or are you struggling by half way through?

You can also ask your "checkers" to complete the Personal Statement Checking Form in Appendix 2 of this book.

It's important that you choose "checkers" who will be honest with you: stress that you're looking for brutal feedback, not faint praise. This is the time when you're looking for constructive and critical commentary in order to help you improve it, not the time to make you happy by telling you it's wonderful when it isn't. At the same time, you must be ready to receive this feedback! If the feedback you're being given is thoughtful and constructive, be prepared to listen to it. This is why you asked them in the first place.

Who should you ask? Generally having two checkers is the optimum number (although for the sake of family harmony, if they're both around and willing, count your parents as one).

More than two and you risk conflicting advice and twisting your statement to try to appease a small army of critics. Fewer than two and you may miss out on good ideas and advice.

Assuming that you have no choice than to let your parents read it (although try to avoid having it passed around the whole family), it's also good advice to let a trusted teacher or university counsellor read it. Teachers and counsellors will have seen many statements over the years and should have a good idea of what universities are looking for in a Personal Statement. Whilst well-meaning, parents may not have as much experience in the university applications process and may be less aware of exactly what your Personal Statement needs to do and show (if in doubt, feel free to pass them a copy of this book to read!).

All said and done however, it's your Personal Statement, and you should be able to trust yourself. Take feedback and critique on board politely and respectfully, but if you choose not to follow it, that's also your decision and your right with your Personal Statement.

Step 5 Summary – The Importance of Editing

Although somewhat laborious and technical, the process of editing your statement is essential to ensuring that it represents your best work, and the best you. Begin by self-checking and self-editing. Be sure that you're not making careless mistakes in your spelling and grammar that you really should be avoiding. Be as critical as possible of your work. Yes you can be proud of it, but don't risk ruining a great Personal Statement by getting careless and sloppy at the final hurdle. If your spelling and grammar is sound, check it for monotony and the common over usage of words such as "I". When it comes to reducing your word count, it's more than OK to be ruthless with the niceties. Your focus should be on making your Personal Statement as clear and concise for the reader as possible, and whilst you don't want to remove any essentials, you certainly can remove anything that doesn't fully support what you're trying to say, is unclear, or is simply redundant. Once all of that is done, get it checked. Checked? Edit and then check it again yourself.

A call to action

You're reaching the end of your Personal Statement journey. If you've given it the required space between writing your first draft and beginning the editing process, you're free to start editing.

Begin by conducting your own checks on spelling and grammar, as well as restructuring any sentences that you think could be changed to improve the flow. Once you've mastered that, ensure that it fits into the 4000-character limit by ruthlessly deleting anything extra or erroneous. Once you think it's as good as you can make it, pass it over to your designated checkers. You can give them a copy of the checklist in Appendix 2 to help them. Take their feedback on board and decide whether to follow or ignore it. Then final changes, final check, copy it over to the UCAS website, final final check, and you're done!

Book down, go get editing!

CONCLUSION

There we have it. If you've followed the guidance in each chapter carefully, you should now have a high-quality UCAS Personal Statement sitting in front of you. You have permission to be pleased with yourself. You have permission to be proud of it. You have permission to take 10 minutes off and go and make a nice hot cup of tea.

From Step 1 you'll have identified exactly what it is that the admissions officers are looking for not just in any Personal Statement, but in your Personal Statement. You'll know the skills, qualities and attributes you need to show alongside your passion for the subject and you'll have been able to use these to create a uniquely crafted and laser-focused Personal Statement.

The structure and examples you worked out in Step 2 will have been carefully chosen to bring these skills to the fore in your statement, whilst the reflections and learning points you wrote about in Step 3 will take these examples to the next level. Your authentic and considered reflections will by now be proving you to be a highly insightful and intellectual individual who is ready to take the next steps on your academic journey at university.

After putting it all together in Step 4, you'll have crafted winning introductory and closing paragraphs, as well as avoided some of the most common pitfalls and clichés that first time and uninitiated first-time Personal Statement writers fall into. Your paragraphs will be clear and succinct, and your language fresh and readable.

Finally, in Step 5 you'll have undertaken the process of editing and perfecting your statement, from improving your grammar and style to reducing the word-count and enlisting trusted helpers to cast their eyes over it.

Your Personal Statement is finally complete. You're ready to upload it to UCAS. You're ready to send your university application. You're ready to start receiving offers from universities of your choice. You're ready to begin any future you choose.

Good luck.

Appendix 1: Complete Personal Statement Examples

These Personal Statements were all written by real students and have been included here, with their permission and without any alterations – exactly as they were submitted to UCAS. Each of these students received either 4 or 5 offers from the universities that they applied to. Feel free to read them for inspiration but remember not to steal their ideas!

Engineering – by Amy

Scientists discover the world that exists; engineers create the world that never was. It is this application of science to the world that excites me so much about engineering; from daily life applications such as how watches work, to amazing feats of human engineering like aeroplanes and skyscrapers. Recently, as part of an extracurricular project, I was part of a team of 3 who designed and built a scale model of a wooden bridge. We were challenged to minimize the cost of building the bridge whilst still making it stable. This project changed my understanding of real world engineering; previously I had just considered the beauty of the bridge, but now had to consider the realistic factors of cost and stability. It is challenges like this that draw me to engineering. I want to be able to design and build the world around me, I want to be the designer of my life.

I have always been a strong student in mathematics and physics and have received exceptional grades. This has always come naturally to me because of the enjoyment and sense of accomplishment I get from these subjects. To be able to solve problems in different ways, for example the many different approaches to integrate an equation, through U-substitution or through integration by parts, keeps me engaged and always exploring new possibilities.

One particular area of interest for me is the problem of clean energy. As burning fuels does nothing but create pollution problems, I want to be able to contribute to helping to tackle this challenge. As such, for my IB Extended Essay I investigated the efficiency of solar panels, studying the effects of different wavelengths of light on photovoltaic cells. Although my experiment failed at first, redesigning it taught me about the importance of thoroughness and clarity in my thinking processes and the importance of listening to critical feedback in order to improve and succeed. I also learnt a lot from my conclusion being different to my hypothesis. I had hypothesised that purple coloured light would produce more electricity, but in fact, it was orange light that produced the most. My hypothesis was wrong because I had not taken into account the limitations of the absorption ability of the cell, but even this has inspired me and taught me that there is always more that I don't know, and more to find out. With this is mind, I am looking forward to being able to study a broad range of engineering modules, in order to gain experience before specialising.

For my work experience I spent 7 days working in an electrical appliance manufacturing plant. In the research and development department I learnt about 3D graphing, whilst at the production lines I learned about how an industrial manufacturing company works, how electrical appliances are made from nothing and the effort and creativity involved in the process. I was particularly interested in their efforts to make their energy use cleaner by turning the heat from the machinery into a water heater, ensuring that no energy was lost.

Having visited several UK university Open Days in the summer of 2016 I am confident that I can adapt to life in the United Kingdom. I am a confident and outspoken person, and have won prizes for my debating skills, as well as reaching the semi-finals of a city-wide public speaking competition. Debate improves my research skills and shows that I am a good communicator and thinker. I have also participated in a wide range of activities outside of normal school life, including developing teamwork through my volleyball team, learning about financial and time management through the organisation of a "Business Bazaar" and whole school "Games Day", and reflecting on my experiences of volunteering once a month at a local autism centre. Studying piano for ten years has taught me about the value of discipline in practising and frequent overseas travel has made me a more open-minded and well-rounded person, who is ready for the challenge of university education in the UK.

Maths and Statistics - by Tim

I am enthusiastic about both the NBA and data; attracted by the fancy moves of basketball stars, but also the relationship between "data points". For example, the relationship between the field goal percentages of a point guard under certain circumstance and the choices of tactics. This led to a fascination with statistics and applied mathematics. I believe data is a means to an end because the goal of statistics is to discover the rules between two concepts and then use this to predict based on data collection and analysis.

My interest in applications of mathematics led me to use knowledge of operational research for my mathematics IA, where I worked out the most efficient escape routes from school. After working out the time needed for escape, I used the matrix to model the situation related to the speed of students and the width of the staircase. This forced me to go beyond my curriculum and learn about concepts such as Hungarian method, whilst also highlighting the importance of inter-disciplinary studies: I also tried to use the coefficient of diffusion in chemistry when I wanted to add the diffusion of toxic gases in my model. I was engaged with this project as I could apply my mathematical knowledge to real world problems; in China there is a long history of poor evacuation planning that has led to unnecessary deaths, and I was pleased to be able to contribute towards solving this.

To learn more about the use of mathematics in daily life, I interned in the data centre of a large media company to understand the job of an analyst. My colleagues taught me techniques of filtering data with Excel and of the visualisation of data with Tableu. I also used ICT skills with one of my colleague, who majored in applied maths and statistics. During the process of quantifying users' satisfaction in the internet platform of the company, I was inspired that a presentation of data should not only be understandable but aesthetic. I realized the importance of ICT skills for analysts and mathematicians, both for the analysis and the presentation. This led me to studying ICT skills online, and then practicing applying them in my academic curriculum, whether through time-saving coding or presentation skills.

Keen to explore the world of mathematics outside of my academic curriculum, I also participated in maths competitions, being secured Zonal Rank 9 in the finals of International Mathematics Olympiad competition and participating in the Australia maths competition. I was pleased that they showed my improvement in understanding English content and my ability to adapt in a new environment. Having only recently joined an international curriculum and started studying in English, I was proud of the progression I'd made in being able to effectively compete in competitions where the medium of communication was English. I also wanted to inspire others as I believe math can be interesting to everyone, including students who currently found maths boring or difficult. Hence, I set up a program of teaching maths to juniors. During the whole semester, I guided my juniors and solved problems with them every night. Finally, some students performed better than ever and the teacher praised our work. I gained the skills in communication with others as well as collaborative skills. But most importantly, the satisfaction brought by math tutorial, one of my contributions to school, is beyond compare.

To broaden my international education horizons, I visited a wide range of countries. I spent two weeks in Hwa Chong Institution (Singapore), as well as completing summer schools in the USA and Canada, and participating in a tour of more than 10 UK universities. These experiences introduced me to people with diverse cultural backgrounds, making me more open-minded. Furthermore, I became more self-motivated since international education gave more flexibility to students, which is something that inspires me to continue to study internationally in the future.

Business – by Dennis

When reading news analysis from sources like the BBC or China Daily, I am attracted by anything related to business, especially new business models connected with high technology, a simple example of which is Uber in the US and its counterpart DiDi in China. These applications not only make our life more convenient but also solve unemployment issues by creating flexible labour opportunities. I am astonished by how sophisticated such kind of business logic is and I believe that in the 21st century the business model had changed: creativity and innovations are now dominating in the information era. I am curious of how the business market will be in the future as the products nowadays are really unpredictable.

I am skilled at analysis and logical thinking and find that my brain works through creating connections and visualizing relationships: I prefer mind-mapping instead of traditional notes-taking. In maths for example, this helps me to take seemingly separate data sets, and relate them together using mindmaps. This helps me to then infer from the given data step by step and get the results by applying various formulas. Being able to see the whole map together rather than just separate areas is an important skill for Business management, where we need to weigh up the pros and cons of our decisions and see the impacts that they could have on a wide variety of areas.

Moreover, I have even put my critical thinking and business inspirations into practice. When attending the ASDAN World Youth Economic Forum I was tasked to create a business model for a media company. As one of the group leaders, I had a mission to design the business strategy for this company to build up reputation as well as improving the medical conditions in the Middle East. This meant that we had to handle the conflicting aims of earning a profit for the business, whilst also taking into consideration ideas of corporate social responsibility and improving the area in which our business would operate. As a result, we decided a win-win approach would be that with one box of medicine sold, the company would donate one to the Middle East. This would improve the reputation of the firm, helping with our marketing strategy whilst also meeting our social goals. That work actually trained me to be more innovate boldly and be able to communicate with different people from other countries as we all have different cultural background which I think is important to business management.

An ability to learn quickly is also important for academic study and when running a successful business. To learn fast, I often look into opinions that differ from or even contradict with one another, before making a decision. During my work experience in a 5 Star Hotel, I joined almost every brainstorming section involving the recruitment of new employees and found those HR managers often held varied views on a particular candidate. By an intensive discussion, they could analyse all the strengths and weaknesses of the candidate to decide whether he or she fitted the company. So, I think learning from different perspectives is effective and efficient in the long run.

I am a member of a public speaking club, a drama club and an art club. Packed with assignments and tasks both from the school and clubs, these areas of learning helped me to have a more creative mind, yet at the same time become more disciplined. For instance, having to manage so many tasks concurrently has helped me to become more efficient and to use my time more effectively. As the Vice-President of the Art Club, I found that I was able to guide my juniors in developing these skills also, sharing my ideas and experiences. Having studied in an International Education Institution, with many Overseas Education Programmes, including the UK, I am confident in my abilities to adapt to the new environment that studying overseas will bring, and look forward to continue to pursue business management academically.

Marketing – by Fangsiqi Z.

Winning the championship in the "Gamble for Crisis" Business Competition helped to develop my interest in exploring the world of business in depth and motivated me to complete a rewarding internship at Hisense in 2017. During this practice, I was able to participate in the operation of some of the core business by virtue of my solid basis in business knowledge, which deepened my understanding of the significance of effective business strategies in maintaining enterprises' sustainable development. Therefore, I aspire to turn myself into a business talent with an international horizon.

Through my IBDP study, I have been able to develop a strong application ability and critical thinking skills. For instance, in my math internal assessment I proposed an effective way to shorten students' queuing time to deposit money into the meal card through using Poisson distribution to create a mathematical model. This attempt not only testified my competence in statistical analysis but displayed my awareness in customer service as well. Similarly, in my Business IA, I evaluated the international marketing scheme of Hisense by looking at their brand image, financial solvency, brand awareness overseas, and possible risks. Meanwhile, I interviewed the marketing manager and adopted SWOT analysis chart to know more about the pros and cons in sport marketing. While cooperating with the manager and other colleagues, I polished my communication skills.

To upgrade my business understanding further, I interned in the International Marketing Department at Hisense and assisted in their marketing project of sponsoring the 2018 FIFA World Cup. By attending the telephone meetings with overseas partners and finishing the background investigation of four prospective advertising companies in this sponsorship project, I understood what elements should be included in evaluating a marketing project and partner, and research skills (because it is difficult to assess foreign website in China). Moreover, I realized the importance of exploiting new markets and brand promotion. In addition, I learnt how to collaborate with colleges to tackle problems and explore potential solutions.

In the "Gamble for Crisis" Business Competition, my skills in business negotiation and problem solving were refined once more. Our team was the tertiary sector in the competition and our goal was to construct the robots and sell them to the government to earn profits. At the beginning of the contest, we got low profits as one teammate forgot to install the robot's arm, thus our first robot was sold at a low price. To win the game, we managed to convince other teams and groups in the secondary sector to give us a loan at low interest. With the help of these funds, we successfully caught up and won the championship. In this match, 1 learnt that communication, negotiation and networking are crucial for the success of a business.

Out of the school, I am an active figure in various activities that concerns public welfare. From October 2016, together with my classmates, I operated a public social media account - Yolo Shunde on WeChat, a popular on-line social communication platform in China. In this account, we periodically published articles about eating, living as well as healthcare information in Shunde with the aim of helping newcomers to this area. This media practice will underpin my study in marketing too. Based on my observation, online media and communication platforms have become main marketing channels of companies in China. And the statistics we get from these platforms will benefit company's decision to make relevant marketing schemes. I also frequently participated in charity bazaars. I ever painted a picture which auctioned from a minimum price of 888 Yuan and donated it to a charity organization. I always hold a belief that a successful entrepreneur should possess strong social responsibility.

English and Creative Writing – by Sharon

English, albeit foreign, has always held a great fascination for me. Unlike many of my contemporaries who find English learning tedious and demanding, I read English books for pleasure. The exquisite vocabulary of English and especially how writers use it to depict real or imaginary worlds and plot stories mesmerises me profoundly. Throughout the years of being a diligent literature reader, I came to understand the power of language. Therefore, I wish to learn how to wield the magic of language myself, hoping one day I can build a world of my own using paper and ink, in which people can find beauty, quietude and comfort just as I have in others'. Also, from people like Khaled Hosseini and Lu Xun who have woven politics and humanitarian causes into literature, I discovered that literature can actually make an impact on society in its own poetic way. Therefore, I want to turn my interest in English language and my skill of writing into something more meaningful, and that requires further study in my higher education.

Intellectual curiosity is regarded as a crucial component in the pursuit of almost every discipline and writing my Extended Essay on a classic and long-debated history topic - causes of the First World War - provided me an excellent opportunity to hone skills like research, analysis, refutation and argumentation while never losing the enthusiasm to delve in even deeper. History provokes critical thinking in my study as I need to develop an argument of my own instead of agreeing to whatever I am told. In addition, the process of writing my Extended Essay on History allowed me to read and write more, which aptly serves to improve my English as well.

One of the two literature pieces chosen for my English B HL is 1984 by George Orwell. It is one of the most challenging books I have read, not only because of its sophisticated language but also because of the abstruse political ideologies and philosophies involved. Its level of difficulty did not scare me off but made me learn even harder to reach a higher standard in order to understand the book. It is of a genre I had rarely touched before, and a speech I wrote based on the book led me to explore uncharted territories. I learnt to employ modes of persuasion in my writing and saw my potential in writing argumentative essays. I had been too focused on descriptives during my IGCSE years and deliberately avoided titles that include argumentation. Studying 1984 made me understand that getting out my comfort zone can actually bring surprises, and that in the pursuit of creativity, one should never be afraid to try something different and unfamiliar.

Outside of the curriculum, CAS is where I gave play to my writing ability and creativity. For my CAS project, I created a WeChat Official Account with my peers to promote book reading by posting book reviews. I enjoyed writing the reviews because I got to reflect on what I have learned and gained in each book, and oftentimes the reviewing part was when I learned the most as I tried to extract the essence of the book, present my interpretation of its gist and evaluate the values I obtained from it. This experience significantly helped me to become a reflective learner in other subjects of study too. In another CAS experience, I maintained an online presence on a website called Duitang. I incorporated my love for fragrances with my interest in poetry in a project, reviewing a line of perfumes by writing a short poem for each of them, characterising and personifying each scent with a story. The poems received lots of appraisal on the website Duitang and I again found myself immersed in artistic creation. In general, I gained satisfaction through sharing my aesthetic visions with others in CAS, as I have always viewed writing as a way of expression. In my belief, English, although seen by many as not so vocational a course, prepares me for a broader future as a critical thinker, an innovator and a global citizen.

Liberal Arts - by Cherry

Attending the Harvard Summit for Youth Leaders in China (HSYLC) gave me my first taste of a Liberal Arts curriculum. I realised that I could not define myself as simply a "science person" or an "arts person" as I was fascinated by courses across various disciplines: from a seminar on Practical Electronics to the History of Hip Hop. This motivates me to study Liberal Arts as it is about exploring knowledge itself and will allow me to take interdisciplinary approaches to explore the connections between various disciplines. The exploration will always give me a new perspective towards the world we are live in and enhance my intellectual experiences, helping me to become a better critical thinker and communicator.

I have made inter-disciplinary connections throughout my IBDP study. For example, for my Extended Essay I chose to explore the relationship between Chemistry and Art. When assisting toning colours for art, I was constantly distracted by the acrid smell of dye and was aware that synthetic dye can be toxic to the human body. I decided to use my knowledge of Organic Chemistry to compare the characteristics of azo and natural dye, aiming to improve methods of producing natural dye. During this exploration I was fascinated by the way that the abstract chemical formula of diazonium salts on paper could transfer into a vivid indigo dye after coupling with phenol. From this investigation, what I have learnt is far beyond Chemistry knowledge itself, but more about how to conduct interdisciplinary research. I learnt how to investigate the relationship between two subjects using scientific methods. Similarly, I was keen to combine my mathematical theory with my dance background for my Mathematics IA, to solve the problem of foot deformation due to the pressure on the toes when dancing on pointe. Using differentiation, I was able to minimize the pressure applied and adjust the shape and angle of "the box", thus demonstrating how it is possible for ballerinas to experience less pain. I found this research particularly interesting because it allowed me to apply my theoretical knowledge to solving real-world situations.

Following the HSYLC conference I was selected as one of 46 students to visit Harvard, MIT and Yale where I was able to develop my problem solving and leadership skills as part of the MIT Energy Hackathon. Using a step-by-step process to take the posed problem from abstract idea to practical solution, I particularly enjoyed the thought processes involved and how it forced me to tackle problems from multiple perspectives. One challenge that we faced however, was combining the opinions of the outspoken group leaders; they each made valid points, but misunderstandings and inconsistencies were arising. I acted as a "bridge", organizing proper communications amongst the group members through attempting to understand their thoughts about the conflicts, before convincing them that better communication was needed. This also allowed shier members of the group to be encouraged to express themselves and I realized that being a true leader is not about standing at the top of the pyramid, but to think from a perspective that would benefit the entire group, to cater to each members' potential growth and to convey messages effectively in a group of outstanding leaders.

I have also developed the ability to empathise through a project I founded called "YoloShunde!". "Yoloshunde!" is a micro-blog survival guide to assist foreign expatriates living in my town. To identify and meet their needs, I had to understand their perspectives and culture. I had to think carefully about how to express myself clearly and comprehensibly. It helped me to develop my communication skills not just with our audience, but within our own team also. Through developing teamwork and awareness of different capabilities, we have been able to build a successful platform, and it is these skills that I look to be able to transfer to my study in the UK.

Psychology – by Ally

'As one pursuing knowledge, you must be a risk taker; able to rise to the challenge and never quit'. The words from my teacher have become an inspiration and a mantra I have followed throughout my studies. Before hearing the words, I was seriously stressed about my studies and future direction which made me feel anxious and depressed, leading me to become interested in mental health and psychology as I found methods to cope. I decided to commit to psychology wholeheartedly having seen the benefits it can bring to people through coping with my own stress. This enthusiasm has led me to my dream career goal of being a psychological consultant.

With psychology not available as a school subject, I developed my interest based on my readings and through my other subjects. For example, a psychologist needs strong research skills as well as experimental skills. For my EE, although "unrelated" and about digestive enzymes, I have learned a lot about the process of research. In my understanding, research skills refers to how we identify a question, searching for the information to support our arguments effectively and using it to solve the problem. I began by finding broad based information on enzymes, before narrowing down the topic to digestive enzymes. I developed the research by using different resources including articles, books, and videos. In the process of finding resources, I always make sure the accuracy and reliability of the sources, whilst also filtering unimportant information.

To gain a deeper understanding of psychology and the career

of a psychological consultant, I did work experience in a psychiatric hospital's psychological consultation department. I learnt that consulting psychology required the psychologist to be patient and sincere when they helped patients reduce emotional disorder through communication and self-exploration. In the process of practice consultation with my supervisor, I got to know that even a simple conversation could show much information about the patient when we observed their reactions, expressions and behaviours. I learnt to analyse and explore the reasons behind people's behaviours and characteristics. This experience led me to realize that there were many teenagers like me who suffered from depression and some of them even committed suicide. There were various hidden reasons behind it, relationships with school mates, bullying, family fights, those which would be difficult for teenagers to share with their friends, teachers or families. Compelled to action, I planned a schools' mental health project including an emotional control pamphlet, and stress management workshop in order to increase the awareness of mental health among students: helping them detect when someone needs help or needs to see a doctor.

Beyond this I have explored methods to reduce mental stress both personally and for the benefit of others. Considering ideas about music therapy, I entered a singing competition as I found it was an effective personal stress release that helped calm me down. I also played an active role in a monthly project at an autism centre. Whilst on one hand the activities provided stress-relieving respite for the parents, working with the children in terms of music therapy and counselling reinforced the idea that psychology could help in many different ways; proving to me that this was an area I wanted to explore further.

I have developed leadership and communication skills through other outside projects. Initiating a project to improve the school's recycling system meant that I had to work with a broad range of stakeholders; from managing my student helpers to liaising with the school management. It also helped me to sharpen my research and analysis skills as we investigated the need, analysed the results, and developed a solution. I am confident that these skills and experiences will help me become a promising psychologist in the future.

International Relations – by Temidayo

After 12 years in Singapore, the country my sister and I grew up in, and our family called home, we had to leave because our respective visas would not be renewed. Consequentially, we were faced with forceful deportation in a months' time, and I was prevented from completing my GCE 'O' Level. This experience inspires me to ensure that youths all over the world never worry about having an education because of the passport they hold, nor are disadvantaged by narrow-minded policies of domestic politics.

To prepare myself for the rigor of my future degree, I have seized any opportunity to improve my critical thinking skills and investigate issues that drive me. As a Nigerian who grew up in Singapore, and is currently living in China, I used my Chinese Written Task to tackle the question "Where is home?". The essay allowed me to reflect on what it means to be a third culture kid - the responsibility to bridge relationships between cultures. To sharpen my analytic skills, for one of my History IAs, I investigated the failure of the United Nations over the Rwandan Genocide. This was by comparing multiple sources and testing them for reliability to build up a concrete picture of the situation. By examining sources from different perspectives, I have been intrigued by the issue of whether it is even possible to establish absolute blame, and the influence of perception and standpoint in historical documentation: an idea that will be directly relevant to the study of International Relations.

With the aim of analysing how works of fiction highlight historical and political realities, I chose English as the subject of my EE. I researched how the portrayal of search of personal identity by Kambili and Jaja, from "Purple Hibiscus", allude to the political struggles of post-colonial Nigeria. The exploration unlocked a new value of fictional work to me - interesting the masses to gain knowledge in historical studies and motivating them to stand up for their right to political freedom. Likewise, I do not shy away from any chance to prepare myself for the major outside my studies and have been rewarded with improved problem-solving abilities. Last February, I spent 7 days in a Human Resources department for my work experience. There, I wrote a proposal in Chinese for an event to help foreigners new to Shunde settle in well. The internship opportunity allowed me to improve my communication skills and sharpened my ability to think from multiple perspectives.

In addition, I took part in a Guangdong province wide MUN competition. For the first round, my essay on the topic of populism put me in first place. I discussed the reasons for rising populism, gave solutions to combat it, and learnt how terrorism is an issue that the world has been struggling with for a long time. I also learnt how difficult it truly is to kill an ideology. In the second round, my speech and debate skills put me in second place. I discovered how important it is to be articulate, and open to opposing perspectives. Another rewarding competition I took part in was The Queen's Commonwealth Essay Competition. In my essay, I gave my take on peace - governments prioritizing too the innocence of foreign youths who call their country home when creating policies. The experience not only helped me grow as a writer, it also gave me the opportunity to reflect on the way I see the world.

My CAS projects and experiences too highlight my interest in my future major. Together with some friends, we founded YEAH! Recycling, a project to motivate students to be more environmentally conscious. As the leader, I not only created awareness of the dangers of non-biodegradable products but also introduced new and creative ways to make recycling part of everybody's daily life. The experience not only taught me the importance of effective communication, creative thinking, but also that the world needs immediate collective effort to solve the issues of Global Warming before it is too late.

Computer Science - by Paul

I started to interact with Computer Science, especially programming, when I was selected in primary school to participate in a competition. Although the software we were competing on, named PC Logo, is very simple when I look back on it, I still learnt one thing from the repeated trying and failing – and it is probably the most basic and the most important thing for programmer – never give up, the next time will always have a greater chance to succeed. For me the most impressionable moment during the preparation for the competition occurred when, after struggling with the process of formulating the programme, we finally managed to get it to match the requirements. The sense of accomplishment from solving logical problems such as this inspired me to seek out further challenges involving logic and reasoning. However, I did not become interested in Computer Science, and programming specifically, immediately after the competition, but actually in 2014 when I found my interest, and indeed my talent, in mathematics.

As a student who excels in Mathematics I was excited to be able to conduct a thorough Mathematical investigation as part of my Extended Essay. Initially I wanted to be able to apply mathematics to the game of tennis and investigate how mathematics can be used to find the optimal position a player should stand in order to prevent an ace from being served. However, upon realising that my proposed method of trial and error would not be precise enough to gather accurate results, I adapted my plans to use mathematical modelling in order to cover for all eventualities that would not be taken into account through trial and error. Having to change my plans and method taught me about the importance of preparation and thinking ideas through carefully and systematically in order to gain more efficient, error free results.

For me, the application of mathematics is much more interesting than finding new mathematical theories. In 2014 I learnt some of the basics of the Visual Basic for Applications from my classmate, and I found my enjoyment in imagining the running of the programme when I was writing it. The feeling I think is just like how a mother feels when she is pregnant, imbued with joy after the programme worked successfully, and like nothing can stop me.

I was fascinated – again – by the programme used during an ASDAN business competition that I competed in in 2016. The programme stimulated trading, by analysing and comparing every market decision made by all of the companies involved, and I was deeply fascinated by the series of algorithms in the programme to process the numbers inputted. After the competition, I collected as many reports as possible from each round of the stimulation and began to deduce the algorithms that would result a similar outcome after calculation. Although at the time I lacked the knowledge to build a programme of my own, I remain intrigued by the concept and plan to explore the issue further.

Although my passion for mathematics has influenced my choice of CAS activities during my IBDP; projects have included teaching Grade 7 students Mathematics and Microsoft Excel, as well as organising an inter-house Maths Competition, I also have a broad range of other interests and experiences. As a member of the Student Council Executive

Committee I have been involved with the organisation of many school events, from leading a group in designing the decor of our school Christmas party to spearheading an investigation into how we could improve the initiative and flexibility of our Student Council members. This was important for me in using my leadership and teamwork skills, teaching me that it is not possible for a team to be outstanding, unless all of its members contribute to the hard work.

Indeed, it is this idea that being outstanding requires hard work that has become a guiding principle of my life, and one that I am certain ensure future success at university and beyond.

Economics – by Selina

Products in chemistry can be obtained by predictable reactions. Number in mathematics can be calculated through fixed formula. Inflexible knowledge like this does not catch my attention. It is the uncertainty and unpredictability of the economy that excites me so much about economics and finance; from the simplest phenomenon such as how demand and supply affect prices of goods, to complicated macroeconomic models like Keynesian theory. For example, as part of the ASDAN Mathematics Tournament I was invigorated by the estimation round. We had to estimate values accurately through given information such as calculating American's GDP given the population of 321 million in 2015. Although estimations can never be wholly accurate, being able to make them is an essential skillset for the running of large companies or even countries. This competition refreshed my understanding of the real-world economy. Previously, I had thought that economics was limited to economic theories and the current economy but have now realized that the importance of applying estimation and other subjects to the future economy, as the effects of the economy can be felt in all areas of life. It is challenge and complexity like this that drives me into economics and finance.

For my Economics Internal Assessment, I researched the growth in American employment over the past 2 years, particularly the spike of March 2017, despite slow economic growth. According to theory, employment should increase faster with stronger economic growth, but this did not fulfil the real-life situation. What happens in reality may not exactly meet the theory I have learned. This made me look for other causes until I found that business confidence also encourages employment. It taught me to think critically when facing uncertain situations, which I found was indispensable in analysing economics problems. It is this critical and analytical thinking that drives me to explore further in economics, where I have realised that my current knowledge is only a stepping-stone into unlimited horizons.

For my work experience, I worked in the Ramada Plaza Hotel in Shunde, China. Service industries such as hotels are flourishing in China nowadays. Based on my daily observations, I noticed that there were not many customers in the hotel which roused my curiosity as to how it can survive in this highly competitive market. Through communicating with colleagues, I realized that Ramada Plaza has monopolistic power in our town because it is the highest-grade hotel. With strong brand image, it attracts many members of the high-income groups to consume here, therefore generating a high revenue from a limited customer base.

I also maintain a healthy interest in news about the economy. I owe my interest to my father. As a banker, he pays special attention to the news of rising interest rates and stock market quotations. Instead of just watching news, we discuss the consequences of these actions and their effects on our lives. This exposure to serious discussions of real economic problems in my family has gradually matured my understanding of the world. Moreover, reading this news broadens my horizon about the economy. In this hyper-competitive era, personal traits are highly valued alongside knowledge. Through organizing the inter-house math competition in school, I have learned to delegate and to lead in an event. As a leader, I was in charge of the event flow, including the design of activities and consultation with teachers and senior students. This taught me that the success or failure of team work hinges on the extent of cooperation, which is also an invaluable quality in financial sector.

With a long way to go in my study in economics and finance and an understanding of my limitations and weakness, I am looking forward to studying in the UK to further equip myself with knowledge and skills. I confidently believe that I can make progress and contributions to the university.

Medicine – by Sriyansh

Not all superheroes wear capes, but they all take oaths. The Hippocratic Oath is astonishing as it places emphasis on ethics over science and even though it is for doctors, its principles can be applied to daily life. It shows the significance of the human touch and that is why I want to do medicine as opposed to other science subjects. The different types of oaths also show the complexities of human life but are all based on caring "adequately for the sick" giving me further insight into the intricacy of the profession as I can bring my own perspective and develop myself.

As a science student, I am inspired by the scientific aspects of the medical profession, and particularly interested in how they can be improved and advanced for today's world. For my IBDP Extended Essay I explored the best reactants to make aspirin synthesis greener. Experimenting with acetyl chloride, acetic acid and ethanoic anhydride, I was looking to produce a reaction that maximised atom economy as well as see which of the reactants was the safest. Causing a small explosion when I underestimated the reactivity of acetyl chloride, this taught me to be more cautious and methodical in approaching experiments and chemicals and emphasized the importance of thorough preparation.

During a work attachment I learnt about how stethoscopes can be used to detect bruits which could be due to atherosclerosis. I found this particularly interesting as it was something I had learnt in biology and was keen to apply my theoretical scientific knowledge to the real world. This helped me focus my studies as I was able to make connections and see how what I was learning could be applied in my studies and beyond.

I am keenly aware of the importance of maintaining dignity and respect in the medical profession. For example, when working with a male doctor who needed to perform cardiography tests on Muslim women, he asked his female nurse to assist in revealing their torsos. I was impressed by how he handled what could be an awkward situation, and at the same time managed to remain comforting and sensitive by continuously talking to the patient. He advised me on trying to make the patients laugh to ease their tension and act as a counter to the stress, which was something that I then tried to practice during my regular visits to elderly care homes. I recognized my growth when I started to talk more through actions than words. I noticed that the smallest actions often had the greatest impact, simply smiling and talking to them would bring a smile to their face, whilst our heavily planned activities could easily fall flat.

Keen to push my academic experiences further and beyond my curriculum, I've also taken an online course in nursing which has helped me learn about the different sectors of healthcare and the different problems of it. One highlight was the importance of triage, and how the medical professionals have to face difficult ethical questions and make tough decisions: knowing that the loudest patient is rarely the one that's most injured and putting those pressures to one side in order to treat the person that needs them most.

The idea of having to work in high pressure situations was reinforced during my time at a dental clinic. At one point, when juggling a constant stream of patients whilst also needing to sterilize equipment, I learned the importance of maintaining patience and calm, after rushing to go home and accidentally poking myself while emptying a used needle. Knowing that these were skills I needed to develop, I intentionally put myself into a leadership position in a project called "Saving the Arts". Knowing that I would have to manage students from all over the school and maintain constant communication with teachers whilst also juggling planning and schoolwork helped me to experience and practice these essential skills for the future. Similarly, this project helped me to improve my time management and communication.

Appendix 2: Planning and Writing Worksheets

Referred to in the Calls to Action at the end of each chapter, these worksheets are designed to help you in organising your ideas, your examples, your reflections and your checkers.

A4 downloadable versions for printing are available at:

www.personalstatementmethod.com

Worksheet 1: Understanding your course

What subject am I applying for?

	Which university?	Name of course	What skills are they looking for?
1.			
2.			
3.			
4.			
5.			
6.			
7.			
8.			

The Personal Statement Method

Worksheet 2: Organising Your Experiences

Academic Examples	Super-curricular Examples	Extra-Curricular Examples
1.	1.	1.
2.	2.	2.
3.	3.	3.
4.	4.	4.
5.	5.	5.

The Personal Statement Method

Worksheet 3: Reflections

Authenticity Questions to Ask Yourself:	
Overall Experience: • Are my thoughts about the experience mostly positive or negative? What makes them this way? • How did this experience impact my thoughts on the subject? • How did the experience impact those around me? • How was this experience relevant to the real-world or other areas of my life? **Successes:** • Did I meet my goals? What helped me most in achieving this? • What strengths can I identify as having helped me to achieve success? **Challenges:** • What was challenging about the experience? What did I find most difficult? • What did I find hindered progress the most? • Is there an area that I was weak in that I would be able to improve?	**Teamwork and collaboration:** • How well do I feel that I worked with others during this experience? • What were things that my team mates or I did to help to overcome obstacles? **Learning points:** • What was the most important thing I learnt from this activity? • If I had to do it again, would I do it the same way or differently? Why? • After this experience, what's the one thing about myself that I would like to improve? • How will I use what I've learnt on this experience in the future? You don't need to use all questions for all of your examples. Use them as a guide to start your reflective process.
Example: Reflection: Skills highlighted:	Example: Reflection: Skills highlighted:
Example: Reflection: Skills highlighted:	Example: Reflection: Skills highlighted:

Example:	Example:
Reflection:	Reflection:
Skills highlighted:	Skills highlighted:
Example:	Example:
Reflection:	Reflection:
Skills highlighted:	Skills highlighted:
Example:	Example:
Reflection:	Reflection:
Skills highlighted:	Skills highlighted:
Example:	Example:
Reflection:	Reflection:
Skills highlighted:	Skills highlighted:

Personal Statement Checking Form	Yes	No	If yes, where?
Spelling, grammar, and language			
Can you see any spelling or grammar mistakes?			
Can you identify where I've written one word, but you suspect I meant another?			
Can you identify any tense errors or inconsistencies?			
Clarity, meaning and focus			
Is there anywhere you are not clear about what I mean?			
Are there any examples that you don't think truly express the point I was trying to make?			
Are there any examples that aren't fully explained in terms of what I learnt?			
Is there anywhere that you feel it lacks focus on my course?			
Is that anywhere that you need more information to understand what I'm saying?			
Is there anywhere where it gives too much information?			

To what extent does my Personal Statement....	Small Extent	Large Extent
Show my passion for the course I'm applying for?		
Interest and engage you from the beginning to the end?		

Is there any other feedback that you'd like to give?

Acknowledgments

Thank you to my students, those who allowed me to use their Personal Statements as samples, and those who have acted as my guinea pigs over the years in coming up with the method.

Thank you to my colleagues, who've been there to bounce ideas and to check that I wasn't descending into madness.

Thank you to my parents, who've consistently nagged me to get this finished.

Thank you to Minjoo, without whom, not much gets done.

About the author

Alex J Bent is an International Educator who specialises in supporting international students and their families to build their own futures through university and Higher Education.

Guiding students in their planning, portfolio building, and applications, Alex has a strong track-record of working with a diverse range of individuals to successfully apply and enrol in not just the best universities, but their best-fit universities. This has seen students successfully receive offers from the "big names" such as Oxford, Imperial College London, and University College London, but also from niche and specialist courses in areas as diverse as Hospitality Management, Music and Fashion Marketing. Alex also derives strong satisfaction from working with less traditionally academic students and helping them to enable themselves to discover their potential.